Staten Island
IN THE
Nineteenth Century

Staten Island

IN THE

Nineteenth Century

FROM BOOMTOWN TO
FORGOTTEN BOROUGH

JOSEPH BORELLI

Foreword by Borough President James Oddo

THE
History
PRESS

Published by The History Press
Charleston, SC
www.historypress.com

First published 2022

Manufactured in the United States

ISBN 9781467150293

Library of Congress Control Number: 2022931445

Notice: The information in this book is true and complete to the best of our knowledge. It is offered without guarantee on the part of the author or The History Press. The author and The History Press disclaim all liability in connection with the use of this book.

To my sons, no matter where life takes you,
Staten Island is always home.

To my constituents, I hope this book makes you all consider the price we pay
for being one of the five boroughs.

Contents

Foreword

Hanging on a wall in the vestibule of my office is a somewhat faded black-and-white photograph of a distinguished-looking gentleman. He is formally posed, wearing a vested suit with a pocket watch slung across his middle and seated in a high-backed chair. With even the briefest of glances, one can recognize that he sat for the photo around the turn of the last century.

The plaque beneath the framed portrait identifies him: George Cromwell. In 1898, Mr. Cromwell became the first president of the newly minted borough of Richmond. In total, there are fourteen such framed photographs on the walls of that room, representing all its past presidents. Sometime after January 1, 2022, my photograph will be up on one of those walls as well.

They are hung in chronological order, and I note the way the style of dress slowly but inexorably changes from decade to decade. But fashion is not really something I care about. What interests me more is not evident in any photograph. What I want to know is how these men, as the chief executive of the least populous borough, coped with the unique problems they faced while in office.

I readily admit that the easiest assumption to make is that Mr. Cromwell, who took office 116 years before I did, likely encountered none of the difficulties presently confronting the borough. Yes, that assumption would indeed be easy to make—but it would be wrong. Incredibly, maddeningly, some of the conditions that might have discouraged Richmond County from agreeing to join the Greater City of New York in the 1890s still exist today.

Certainly, some of them suffered from unique, but temporary, circumstances—wars, a depression and, in the case of my predecessor, Jim Molinaro, a devastating superstorm known as Sandy. And obviously, there have been incredible advances in science and technology over the past hundred-plus years, advances most of these men could never have imagined and with which they never needed to deal.

Of course, the march of time has dictated that whoever has held this job faced different circumstances and challenges; as I said earlier, though, some problems that existed for this Island, even long before the consolidation, still exist today. The report of the Staten Island Improvement Commission of 1871, which the legislature had authorized to study the problems of our Richmond County, sometimes seems weirdly prophetic.

In French, the phrase is *plus ça change, plus c'est la même chose* ("the more that changes, the more it's the same thing"). The deeper you get into this book, the more you will understand this.

The County of Richmond, which in 1898 concurrently became the Borough of Richmond and, in 1975, the Borough of Staten Island, has had issues that remain intractable even to this day. The reasons for this are myriad, but a principal one is that we share little in common with the rest of what was then known as the City of Greater New York. It is likely that we never will.

If you're blessed with the privilege of sitting in "The Chair" in the Borough President's Office, what should always be lurking in the back of your mind is the "Great Law of the Iroquois"—that our most sacred duty is to think seven generations ahead. In making any decision, wrote author Warren Farrell, one must "be aware of whether the decisions we make today will benefit not just ourselves and our children, but our children several generations into the future."

In effect, there is a dual constituency a borough president must serve: the Staten Islanders of today and those of tomorrow. In order to do so effectively, it is crucial that we understand the Staten Islanders of yesterday.

The challenge is this: how to address problems that began in the past by utilizing the technology and finances we possess in the present, while at the same time honoring the responsibility we have to future generations as yet unborn. Many of the issues that cross my desk on a daily basis, here at the end of the second decade of the twenty-first century, result from decisions made by others in centuries past—from action that was taken…and action that was not.

Our history is replete with choices made, great and small. Some of them affected only a handful of people for a brief moment in time; some affect our entire borough to this day. But knowing that history, knowing how we got here, is a critical variable in the decision-making process of the here and now. An emphasis on deliberate thought, with our past keenly considered, is a huge part of the calculus for moving forward.

As Edmund Burke wrote in 1790, "People will not look forward to posterity, who never look backward to their ancestors."

So now let's take a look back.

—STATEN ISLAND BOROUGH PRESIDENT JAMES S. ODDO

Introduction

In 2017, I started jotting down notes as I skimmed, for the third time, the masterpiece entitled *Staten Island and Its People*, by Charles Leng and William T. Davis. Staten Island—and its people, as it were—occupied a great share of my mind as I proudly represented it and them in the State Assembly and City Council, and I knew that I wanted to write a book chronicling the history of my hometown for a modern audience. Two years later, I had a working manuscript of about 120,000 words and more than 1,000 notes. I had created a monster.

The fantastic team at The History Press immediately saw the problem: I had written two completely separate books that just happened to be connected by a chronological timeline. The former bore little resemblance to the later.

The first half became *Revolutionary Staten Island: From Colonial Calamities to Reluctant Rebels*, which was published in September 2020. Its goal was to tell a story that would be exciting to Staten Island's history buffs and anyone interested in painting a picture of the borough throughout its first two hundred years. I hope readers were shocked to learn how unique Staten Island was in the colonial history of the country and its important role during the war.

This book is different. Sure, it is a continuation of the chronology, but it is also meant to frame a new idea. Staten Island fared pretty well in the early republic and throughout its first century, and perhaps we would be better off had we continued on our own and not joined in with the great experiment of urban expansion known as Greater New York City.

Although a whopping 84 percent of Staten Islanders voted to consolidate, the modern reader will soon realize that the hopes and dreams of those who supported the policy never materialized. The long-awaited benefits of the new mega-city didn't come, and in many cases, they are still owed.

Contrast that with Richmond County before 1898. It was a place of expansion and opportunity, of community spirit and optimism. It was a community of immigrants, business magnates, natural beauty and massive factories; in the same moment, it served as a seaside resort, rail hub and the city's repository for the desperate. It had breweries, brickworks and racetracks; military camps, icehouses and trolleys. It was the refuge of world leaders, revolutionaries and the rich. There were fishing, tennis and cricket clubs, and the toughest contests were political.

In short, Staten Island developed like all other thriving American cities and towns in the 1800s. As we look back on its prosperity when it stood on its own, it is my hope that readers begin to imagine what could be achieved by going our own way once again. It's time we reimagine Staten Island as anything but the "forgotten borough." It must reassert itself as one of the largest, safest and most successful communities in the United States—an honor we held throughout the nineteenth century and one we would soon attain through our political independence from city hall.

CHAPTER 1

Richmond Republic

At the conclusion of the American Revolution, no other county in the newborn United States suffered through more time under occupation, and few had spent as much on its front lines under threat of attack. As such, the rebuilding of Staten Island took much time, due, in part, to the lack of true government throughout its duration. The growth and prosperity that eventually occurred in Richmond County in the early nineteenth century was not unique in the United States. What is noteworthy, however, is that this occurred while Staten Island was self-governed, and its citizens saw little need to be affiliated with, or subjected to, the governing powers of New York City. In fact, city officials looked to the Island to solve some of their own problems.

One thing the county did not lose in the Revolution was its population, which stood at 3,838 souls in 1790,[1] 25 percent more than there were in 1771.[2] While it shed many of its most prominent Tory citizens, it was made up for by the large number of soldiers and refugees who opted to remain after the British evacuated.[3]

This new population needed a restoration of public services, but like elsewhere, the county first had to reorganize a government according to the new state constitution. The four towns that existed before the war—Castleton, Northfield, Westfield and Southfield—were officially re-chartered by the state legislature on March 7, 1788, and an election for their municipal offices followed.[4] In prior contests, the county's electors would have turned to their de facto aristocracy, but its Tory landowners like Christopher Billop, owner of the "Conference House," were already resettling elsewhere and wealthy families like the Dongans, descendants of Governor Thomas Dongan, were subdividing and selling parcels for profit.[5] At the Island's first public meeting as part of New York State and the United States, held at the home of Abraham Reckhow at the Old Blazing Star ferry in modern Rossville, Westfield's electors chose supervisors, assessors and "other Necessary officers."[6] They opted for the Whig slate: John Totten, supervisor, and Peter Winant, town clerk. They also elected officers to serve as assessors, inventory takers, road commissioners, highway commissioners, pound masters and damage appraisers.[7] The other original supervisors were Cornelius Corsen, Northfield; Anthony Fountain, Southfield; and a Moravian Church leader, Richard Connor, Castletown. Johannes Van Wagonen and Adrian Bancker, who spent part of the war as British captive while General Howe used his home as a headquarters during the battle for New York, were elected to the State Assembly.[8]

Soon the county was operating. In 1785, the position of overseer of the poor was created, and both Benjamin Larzellier and David LaTourette were elected[9] and tasked with finding lodging in private homes for impoverished families. In 1803, the county purchased property on Richmond Road for its first poor house, but it quickly proved too expensive and unable to accommodate the demand. In 1829, the state legislature authorized a tax levy to purchase a county farm where those housed could work the land.[10]

In 1795, the state legislature also allocated $50,000 toward establishing public schools around New York. Staten Island opened four, listed as Indian Hill, Smoking Point, Wood Row and Bently.[11]

The restoration of justice was a priority as well, since no court sat between September 1775 and May 3, 1784. On that day, the defendant's own home in Richmond served as the courthouse, as the real one was burned during the war. Judge David Mersereau heard the grand jury indictment of Thomas Frost, accused of using profanity.[12] Frost's house ended up being used as the courthouse for eight years before the authorities purchased it and constructed a new building. Another twelve dollars was allocated in 1801 to construct public stocks.[13]

Road construction dates back to the first years of British rule, and the colonial authorities appointed dozens of surveyors to map several throughout the eighteenth century, right up until the outbreak of war.[14] But it was during the early federal period that the two most important roads in the Island's history were planned. Under the personal ownership

Daniel D. Tompkins. *Courtesy of the Library of Congress.*

of Governor Daniel Tompkins, the Richmond Turnpike Company was formed and authorized to purchase land to shorten the stage coach journey from New York to Philadelphia. The toll road would run for eight miles from a spot near the Watering Place, which Tompkins owned as part of his seven-hundred-acre estate on the north shore, through the Island to Long Neck, where it terminated at the edge of a salt marsh. From there, the *New Blazing Star* ferry took travelers to New Jersey.[15] In the twentieth century, this road would be renamed Victory Boulevard.

Around 1836, Henry Seaman designed and constructed the Richmond Plank Road and a wooden drawbridge crossing Fresh Kills at Greenridge. In the period leading up to the Civil War, this was the most important commercial road connecting the farms and factories of the south shore with the north shore ferry landings to New Jersey and Manhattan.[16] The future Richmond Avenue was the Island's major freight road for decades.

STATEN ISLAND IN THE SECOND WAR FOR INDEPENDENCE

The period shaped by the French Revolution and the Napoleonic Wars was extremely profitable for the United States, especially its eastern port cities, as our nation reaped the benefits of Britain and France effectively blockading each other. Exports climbed from $19 million in 1791 to $108 million in 1807, as overall tonnage shipped shot up from 124,000 to 984,000 tons.[17] In Richmond County, tax receipts quadrupled between 1788 and 1811.[18]

To guard the nation's commerce, the Federalist government embarked on a program of naval expansion and fortification of major ports. Richmond's prospering residents favored this protectionist approach, and it was the only county south of Albany to vote for the Federalist candidate against Dewitt Clinton for governor in 1801.[19] It sent Federalists to Albany to represent them in almost every election that decade. Commerce led politics.[20]

In April 1806, the American schooner *Richard* was approaching New York just two miles off Sandy Hook when it was confronted by the sixty-six-gun *Leander*.[21] The British warship was patrolling the waters off New York Bay in order to impress seamen back into British service. *Leander* fired a warning shot across *Richard*'s bow,[22] and a second went through its stern, decapitating a crewman.[23] Newspapers sensationalized the "murder" and claimed that the ship was just a quarter mile off the Hook. The funeral procession included the mayor and Common Council of New York, and every ship in the harbor flew its colors at half-mast.[24]

Similar incidents ensued, and soon the government had to act. The Non-Importation Act and the Embargo Act, both passed in 1807, "protected" American seamen but also devastated American shipping.[25] The impact throughout New York Harbor was felt everywhere, and on Staten Island, county tax receipts fell by nearly 40 percent.[26] Islanders soon resorted to smuggling, an activity they mastered during the Revolution, and their reputation was so well known that as soon as one trafficker was caught in 1807, the newspapers falsely proclaimed him a Staten Islander.[27]

The other noticeable change around the harbor was "fortification fever," which dominated the opinion columns and public debate for years as the federal government digested the inevitability of war.[28] Staten Island became noticeably militarized, and the Fourth of July festivities of 1807 included an out-of-the-ordinary parade of the county's militia through Richmondtown, led by "Captain Guyon, with his troop of light dragoons…mounted, with swords drawn."[29]

The state legislature ordered a defensive plan for the harbor. Ideas ranged from a flotilla to fire ships, floating cannons, or batteries with moveable carriages.[30] The federal government appropriated funds to develop an experimental sunken "torpedoe" plan thought up by steamship pioneer Robert Fulton; they could be mounted strategically across the Narrows and the Long Island Sound. By 1812, they were in operation and working as planned.[31]

The additional fortification of the Narrows was critical. Due to its height and history as a colonial signal station, the Staten Island side would played the dominant part, and some of the original designs had already been furnished by Britain's most famous engineer, Marc Isambard Brunel.[32]

In 1808, a seventeen-gun salute marked the moment "several Gentlemen" from New York and Staten Island "proceeded to lay the foundation stone on a formidable work on the beach near Signal Hill on Staten Island."[33] It was named Fort Richmond in honor of the county, and when completed in 1810, it housed up to ninety-two guns.[34]

By the war's beginning, another 74 guns had been added, and soon, another $125,000, an astonishing number, was allocated to complete the Island's defenses. Earthworks, stone ramparts and batteries were quickly thrown up into a pentagonal fortress with large round towers on top the bluff above Fort Richmond. To the south, two outer batteries called Fort Morton and Fort Hudson were installed and could fire far into Lower New York Bay.[35] Smaller batteries and earthworks were positioned at Prince's Bay and at the old British fortifications above the Watering Place.[36] Had all of the planned naval guns around Staten Island been in place, there would have been more than 220, including 27 massive thirty-two-pounders.[37]

New York's defensive works did prove their worth. During the War of 1812, the British did not attempt a landing or any attempt to penetrate the fortifications. The closest they came was in January 1813, when a British blockading squadron was sighted off Sandy Hook. Instead of approaching the Narrows, they commandeered vessels offshore. The seventy-four-gun *St. Domingo* came within three miles of the coast[38] and the furnaces for heating cannon shot were readied, but the guns remained silent.[39]

Staten Island was strongly garrisoned throughout the war. At its outbreak, Governor Tompkins ordered four artillery and seven infantry companies to camp around the fortifications. At Fort Richmond and Fort Tompkins, quartermaster logs record an additional 550 men. In 1814, after the burning of Washington, D.C., and the attack on Fort McHenry, an additional 2,150 infantrymen were sent along the Staten Island shoreline to prevent a similar incursion in Raritan Bay. Additionally, Tompkins realized that New York's mariners, many of whom were out of work, would be able to serve in a "sea fencible" corps, able to engage any invasion force with a small flotilla or by manning vacant artillery posts. With Congressional authorization, he raised about 1,000 Islanders to supplement the army artillery corps.[40]

In total, close to seventy-eight thousand New Yorkers served in some capacity in the U.S. armed forces during the war.[41] The most prominent Staten Islanders involved in the effort were John Garretson, commander of the county's militia, and the aforementioned James Guyon, a major in the army's First Cavalry Division (and later elected to Congress).[42]

On February 21, 1815, the guns of Fort Richmond fired a cannonade. It was the only time they were fired during the war, and this was done only to mark the signing of the Treaty of Ghent, which took two months to arrive. A *feu de joie* was begun at Governor's Island, and each fort around the harbor successively opened its batteries in celebration.[43]

Notable Residents and Guests

Daniel Tompkins towers above most other New Yorkers born among the first generation of politicians after the nation's founding fathers had retired or passed on. Only Dewitt Clinton, his one-time lieutenant governor, could compare. Tompkins was an early supporter of the Democratic-Republican Party and rose in its ranks from the New York Supreme Court to the Governor's Mansion, before serving as vice president under James Monroe. During his governorship, when the state and federal government's credit was shaky, and although the president himself would not do so, Tompkins had personally guaranteed loans of $1.4 million to the treasury of the United States, securing the money needed for the war.[44] He was a staunch abolitionist when that was unpopular in New York, dating back to his years at Columbia College, where he asked in a pamphlet, "Should not the pure blood of American patriots recoil at [slavery] and reform by…freeing and civilizing the Africans?"[45] As governor, he demanded the legislature end "unjust and cruel bondage" at the opening of the 1817 legislative session,[46] and in two months, he signed a bill emancipating every citizen of New York State in ten years on July 4, 1827.[47]

At the close of the war, Tompkins's personal attention turned toward Staten Island, where he began buying large properties. His first purchase was West Brighton farm from Abraham Crocheron and thereafter several pieces from

Children of Governor D. Tompkins. This picture depicts the first five of eight children of the governor and Hannah Minthorne Tompkins, including Mangle Minthorne Tompkins, their eldest son, on the right. *Courtesy of the New York Public Library digital collection.*

the Mersereau family on Grymes Hill. His most significant acquisition came in 1815 from the Church of St. Andrew, consisting of nearly all the property known as the Duxbury Glebe. There he built a home (which burned in 1874) just south of Fort Place, and along the nearby shoreline of the Watering Place, he formed the village of Tompkinsville.[48] He mapped out a street grid, naming five after his children: Arietta, Minthorne, Griffen, Sarah Anne and Hannah,[49] two of which keep their original names. By his death in 1825, he had accumulated more than seven hundred acres on Staten Island and owned the Richmond Turnpike Company (Victory Boulevard) as well as a thriving steamboat service to Manhattan.[50]

While he was both vice president and a resident of Richmond County, the Tompkins family worshiped at the Dutch Reformed Church of Port Richmond, but they soon donated land and funds to construct an offshoot in Tompkinsville. At its pulpit in 1823, he gave his final public oration.[51] The original site was at the corner of St. Mark's Place and Victory Boulevard and served until the congregation moved in 1863. It is now the Brighton Heights Reformed Church.[52] On August 15, 1824, he hosted the Marquis de Lafayette as part of his reunion tour forty-one years after the end of the Revolution. Tompkins was too ill to give a speech, so Reverend Van Pelt of the Dutch Church made the toast. Lafayette reflected on the success of the young democracy before bidding the guests farewell by saying, "I hope we shall meet in heaven with Washington and the gallant heroes of the American Revolution."[53] The next morning, shops and business closed, as nearly every resident of Richmond County lined the shoreline to cheer the Frenchman as he ferried to New York City.[54]

Tompkins was not the only vice president to spend his final days in Richmond County. Aaron Burr, decades after his famous duel, passed his final years in political exile on the Island. He took residence at the Port Richmond Hotel at 2040 Richmond Terrace, where he was said to take daily visits from Reverend Van Pelt. He also enjoyed frequent drives through New Springville and the Egbertville Ravine.[55]

On September 13, 1836, Burr died at the hotel.[56] A New York newspaper reported, "He breathed his last in the presence of, and his eyes were closed by, a passing stranger—no relative, friend, or clergyman, being in the room at the time."[57] Before his burial at Princeton College, a funeral was held at the Dutch Church and attended by all of Richmond County's notable residents. The rites were given by Reverend Van Pelt, making Burr the second vice president he had eulogized.[58]

After Burr, spending one's time in political exile on Staten Island became somewhat fashionable. Gustave Von Struve, a German revolutionary and writer, avoided execution and fled to Staten Island in 1851 before serving in the Union army in the Civil War. In a house on Richmond Avenue near Graniteville, he wrote his six-volume *Weltgeschichte* (*World History*). At the same time, though for a shorter period, the exiled Hungarian politician and liberator Lajos Kossuth took refuge here and became the second foreigner to address a joint session of Congress, after Lafayette.[59] A procession and dinner were held in his honor at Nautilus Hall, a Tompkinsville hotel built in 1808, which became famous for the political circle that frequented it.[60] In 1851, the failed Polish revolutionary Joseph Kargé also relocated and "was induced to settle in the midst of a circle of superior families on Staten Island with connections in New York City."[61] He went on to fight in the Civil War and eventually became a professor at Princeton University.[62]

"Remember the Alamo" may be an often-recited battle cry in Texas, but it wasn't the case on Staten Island in the mid-nineteenth century. General and

A later photo of the Port Richmond Hotel, where Vice President Aaron Burr died in isolation in 1836. *Courtesy of the Library of Congress.*

President of Mexico Antonio López de Santa Anna visited and resided on Staten Island more than once in his life. The first trip was in 1847 after his defeat at the Battle of Huamantla, when the Mexican government relieved him of his command.[63] Santa Anna was a friend of Gilbert L. Thompson, the son-in-law of Daniel Tompkins, and it was he who saved the general's life by smuggling him from Mexico to Staten Island the second time after his death sentence in 1865. Once safe, Santa Anna pursued two hobbies. The first was gambling on cockfights and three-card Monte,[64] and the second was recruiting and raising capital for his unsuccessful attempts to return back to power in Mexico.[65]

GENERAL D. ANTONIO LOPEZ DE SANTA-ANNA.
PRESIDENT OF THE REPUBLIC OF MEXICO.
By A.Hoffy, from an original likeness taken from life at Vera-Cruz.

General Antonio López de Santa Anna, president of the Republic of Mexico, resided on Staten Island in 1847 and 1865. *Courtesy of the Library of Congress.*

His political endeavors were fruitless, but folklore has it that his dealings with an amateur New York inventor named Thomas Adams ended up giving birth to a modern $19 billion industry. Santa Anna is rumored to have brought with him a large store of *chicle*—a latex produced by the sapodilla tree—which he hoped Adams could help turn into a profitable alternative to rubber. Those attempts failed, and the eleven-time president returned penniless to Mexico. Adams, however, was left with more chicle than he knew what to do with. That is, until the day he saw a young girl in a candy store chewing on a flavored paraffin wax. He called his subsequent invention "Chicklets," and the modern chewing gum industry was born. The American Chicle Company claimed this version of events well into the twentieth century,[66] and modern anthropologist Jennifer Matthews gives credence to the Staten Island origins of chewing gum.[67] However, there is no mention of Santa Anna or his role in Adams's obituary in 1905.[68]

Above all, the foreign exile most well known in his own time and who had the most lasting impact on Richmond County was the Italian nationalist and *Padre della Patria*, Giuseppe Garibaldi. He resided in the county the entirety of his two stays in the United States—the first from 1850 to 1851 and the second from 1853 to 1854.[69] At the time, New York City and its environs had a colony of about three thousand individuals from the territories now part of modern Italy; many were also political dissidents, and several had been Garibaldi's comrades in arms. His arrival in New York Harbor was a celebrated occasion, with many Italians and native-born New Yorkers forming a reception committee.[70]

Yet, for the most part, Garibaldi's exile in the United States was a melancholy affair. His mind was set on Italy, but the funding for his endeavor failed to materialize. To earn an income, he took residence with one of his former officers, Antonio Meucci, then a candle maker who rented a small house and factory in Rosebank. The general was grateful but unsatisfied, and his allies petitioned the U.S. president unsuccessfully for an appointment to the post office. Although he had many friends, including intellectuals like William Cullen Bryant and Henry Theodore Tuckerman, his scant knowledge of English left him largely isolated.[71] His pleasures included sailing and fishing from a small boat whose sail he painted red, white and green. He also enjoyed hunting and was issued fines on Long Island for violating town ordinances against it. On Staten Island, he was often seen promenading with friends along Richmond Terrace or playing Bocce along the shorefront just north of Von Briesen Park.[72]

Garibaldi left for a lengthy excursion to South America to fundraise for his return to Italy. He revisited Staten Island on his second return, but his stay was brief.[73] His friend Antonio Meucci would eventually claim to be the original inventor of the telephone, and the home they once shared would be moved a short distance to its present location on Tompkins Avenue and preserved as a memorial to Garibaldi first by the Garibaldi Society and then by the Order Sons of Italy in America. It now operates as the Garibaldi-Meucci Museum.[74]

Fine arts found a welcome place on Staten Island as well. Jasper Francis Cropsey, a leading painter of the Hudson River School, was the oldest child born to Jacob Rezeau Cropsey and Elizabeth Cortelyou in 1823 on a farm near Rossville[75] along Arthur Kill Road. A contemporary map places it roughly at the spot of modern Owl Hollow Park.[76] From there, where the family grew grain and vegetables, it would be possible to see the Arthur Kill. He wrote of the view to his wife of in 1850, saying, "You know, over beautiful verdant meadows, and fruit orchards, and the river made cheerful by sails and steamers passing to and fro…and over those white houses, fields of grain, hills, woods, and distant low blue mountains."[77] Today, the view is of Fresh Kills Landfill.

Cropsey's early years were fraught with poor health, and he taught himself to paint while convalescing. His early experiments in oil include rough sketches of the family farm in 1843, depicting it as part of a small collection of buildings set back from the fence line.[78] A more famous work from the same year, now housed in the collection of the Staten Island Historical Society, was entitled *Cortelyou Farm Greenridge*. It depicts his mother's family farm along Arthur Kill Road, near its intersection with the street that still bares their name.[79]

Cropsey's early success was in architecture. On Staten Island, he designed St. Luke's Episcopal Church in Rossville based on sketches he'd seen of the parish church at Ross Castle in Scotland. It lasted one hundred years and was closed[80] and demolished by 1961,[81] and it now serves as a parking lot for the Old Bermuda Inn.[82]

The other church he designed still stands. The Cortelyou family were some of the earliest Moravians to land on Staten Island in the eighteenth century and helped to found its first church in New Dorp. The Moravian community was a large part of Cropsey's early life. He is even often incorrectly cited as buried at the family plot in its cemetery.[83] There is no doubt that it was a source of pride to receive the commission to design its newer and larger home. The young architect chose a Greek Revival structure that reflected the austerity of the sect, and other than an alteration to change the bell tower into a steeple, the church looks much the same as it did when he completed it.[84]

By his death, Cropsey had grown wealthy, and the worldwide popularity of the Hudson River School had earned him enough money to purchase large estates in the Hudson Valley.[85] His Staten Island roots were never far from his thoughts, however, and on several occasions, it provided the subject of his paintings. *Looking Oceanward from Todt Hill* (1895) depicts a scene still familiar to anyone looking out from the Richmond County Country Club; it was a view that he replicated just three years later in *View of Staten Island* (1898). An earlier work is likely the most well-known landscape of the Island, *The Narrows from Staten Island* (1868), which captures the view approximately from where Casa Belvedere now stands and depicts the town of Stapleton in the background behind a small group of people on a hill, one of whom is a self-portrait of Cropsey, painting.[86] In total, Staten Island's native artist created twenty-five scenes of the county in his lifetime, including Ward's Point, Prince's Bay, Richmond Hill, the Narrows and Grymes Hill.[87]

In the 1830s, a giant of American literature also called Staten Island a temporary home. Henry David Thoreau was raised in Concord, Massachusetts, where he became the companion of an equally notable Ralph Waldo Emerson. The two developed a bond, and Emerson, who was thirteen years older, assumed the role of a mentor figure to the young writer. It was he who suggested that Thoreau tutor the children of his brother, Judge William Emerson, who owned a house called The Snuggery atop a hill he named Emerson Hill.[88]

Thoreau spent most of 1843 teaching William Jr. and using his days off to connect with publishers in Manhattan. Soon, William's two younger brothers and a neighbor joined the class, and their tutor took them on long, rambling walks around the Island. In the evening, he explored the county on his own, sending descriptive letters back home.[89] To his sister Sophie, he penned:

The whole island is like a garden, and affords very fine scenery. In front of the house is a very extensive wood, beyond which is the sea, whose roar I can hear all night long, when there is no wind.... There are always some vessels in sight—ten, twenty, or thirty miles off and Sunday before last there were hundreds in a long procession, stretching from New York to Sandy Hook, and far beyond, for Sunday is a lucky day.[90]

Economic Progress

On a spring day in 1825, a Chesapeake schooner rounded Sandy Hook and sailed into Raritan Bay. It was heavily laden with freight but did not put in for shore. Instead, it anchored about a mile off Prince's Bay on a sandbank called Round Shoals, where it unloaded its live cargo into the seabed. That fall, the crew returned on flatboats and raked delicious four-inch oysters for the hungry mouths of New York City. Staten Island's oyster industry had begun.[91]

Raritan Bay always had oysters. They were a staple food for the Lenapes and helped feed the blossoming colony. The colonial governments of New York and New Jersey even protected stocks by banning commercial harvesting during the eighteenth century,[92] and Staten Island residents were appointed to "search & seize" any foreign fishing boats caught transgressing in its coastal waters.[93]

The practice of transplanting "seed" oysters—whether Chesapeake, Blue Point or otherwise—and harvesting them after one year changed the dynamic of oystering and birthed one of county's earliest industries.[94] In Richard Bayles's 1887 Staten Island history, he claimed that "all the men on the southern half of Staten Island may be called oystermen," as nearly everyone spent at least part of their time harvesting.[95]

The full economic benefit of oystering was most evident in the county's southernmost tip. John Totten first purchased land on the south shore in 1767 from Christopher Billop, owner of the Conference House and its vast estate. After the war, Totten's sons, Gilbert and Joseph, emerged as prominent citizens in the town of Westfield and helped found the Woodrow Methodist Church. Gilbert settled in the northeastern corner of modern Tottenville (roughly Page Avenue), where he and his wife had eight children. Their son, John Bodine Totten, had twelve children of his own, and most remained in the area. John Totten Jr., along with his brothers James and William, built a dock to support the burgeoning oyster industry at the foot of Main Street

Oysters were a staple of New Yorkers' diets, often sold from stands like the one depicted in this drawing of Fulton Market in 1870. Tottenville flourished as their popularity grew. *Courtesy of the New York Public Library.*

around 1835, and around that, the town of Tottenville sprang up. By 1850, it claimed dozens of homes, a church, a school and a second oyster dock to keep up with the growing trade. Three years later, a map of Staten Island referred to the small hamlet around Totten's Landing as "Totensville."[96] It was a town built on the oyster trade.

With the opening of the Erie Canal in 1825, all but guaranteeing New York Harbor's commercial dominance, Staten Island was poised to grow as part of the broader trend of industrialization in the Northeast. The county, financially intertwined with New York City if not governmentally, was able to keep pace with the region's progress and soon became the home of numerous industrial outfits.

In 1819, the firm of Barrett, Tileston and Company purchased the Van Buskirk Mill and opened a printing and dying works. In five years, 150 workmen were employed, and the factory and adjacent housing formed the village of Factoryville (now New Brighton). Soon, thousands of new workers populated the north shore in a dozen other enterprises.[97]

Factoryville saw its first gun manufacturer open up between modern Franklin and Lafayette Avenues by Joseph Hall in 1833. In 1835, the India Rubber Cloth Company was formed by Charles Goodyear, the inventor of vulcanized rubber,[98] and of its product the *Richmond County Mirror* praised the Island's "fine specimens…superior to the fabrics manufactured elsewhere."[99]

To the west, the Staten Island Whaling Company formed an oil factory near the old Dutch Church and Decker's Ferry, sowing the shorefront village of Port Richmond. Soon, the Jewett White Lead Works followed in 1842. Even further, the Newton Flour Mill became the first operation in present Mariner's Harbor. On Jewett and along Ocean Terrace on Todt Hill, more than 300,000 tons of iron and minerals were extracted from mines since abandoned,[100] and the granite quarried throughout the north shore was called "the most pure, perfect and indestructible of building materials."[101]

The Island was also expanding the number and type of skilled trades and products. An 1833 *Richmond County Free Press* displayed advertisements for about eighty-five separate businesses, including clockmakers, ship joiners, wood carvers, portrait engravers, furniture makers, tobacconists, cabinetmakers, ballast masters, shoemakers, hardware stores, undertakers, printers, bakers, jewelers and attorneys.[102]

Yet despite the change, farming still remained the dominant profession in the decades before the Civil War. About 30 percent of Staten Island's workforce was employed in agriculture, compared to the 28 percent who worked in manufacturing and 24 percent in maritime trades.[103] In 1842, the New York Agriculture Society published a report outlining the county's production. Indian corn, potatoes, oats, wheat, rye, barley and buckwheat were the principal crops, and it was home to 2,517 head of cattle, 3,180 pigs and 136 sheep.[104]

Interestingly, despite the influx of new residents and the county's overall commercial growth, its real estate values plummeted. While land sold on average for $100 per acre after the War of 1812, by the 1840s, prices of $50 to $70 were more common.[105] This drop can be attributed to the success of the canal in opening up eastern markets to larger farms out west. For Staten Island, the dip meant the birth of a business that would shape the county's progress through to the present day and into the foreseeable future: real estate speculation.

Minthorne Tompkins, son of the governor, partnered with William J. Staples to purchase extensive lands south of Tompkinsville in 1833. They subdivided the property and laid out a road grid. At a soiree on July 23, 1836, the developers toasted their new town, christening it Stapleton.[106] An auction notice went out for 109 lots in the new community, boasting that it had already contained eighty new dwelling units and "a permanent well conducted ferry" to New York.[107] Within five years, it was booming.

At the same time, Thomas E. Davis purchased tracts along the north shore waterfront under a corporation called the New Brighton Association. With deep-pocketed backers like Henry Stebbins and August Belmont, he hoped to duplicate the luxury of the English seaside resort of the same name.[108] The association's plan failed to materialized after a recession in 1837, but the street grid for New Brighton, its subdivisions and some of its early buildings would last to the present day.[109]

The grid plan of Richmondtown was laid out in 1836 by Henry Seaman,[110] and an 1853 map shows a cluster of about thirty buildings around St. Andrew's Church. The same map shows that the north shore was far more densely settled than the south shore.[111] Outside Tottenville and Rossville, there were few clusters of buildings in present-day Charleston, Pleasant Plains, Huguenot (then called Bloomingview) and along the bay.[112] On the east shore, small communities called Clarendon and Oceana encircled Great Kills Harbor and Oakwood Beach, several farms and orchards surrounded the fortifications at the Narrows and a near continuous line of houses stretched along modern Richmond Road.[113] On the West Shore, the small town on the Long Neck at the end of the Richmond Turnpike, then called Chelsea, had sixty-four buildings, nearly all owned by members of the Decker and Pratt families.[114] Farther north, the Van Pelts owned the majority of homes in Old Place, near "Holland's Hook," while to the east there was a cluster of homes around the granite quarry called Granite Village. South along the Plank Road, at the point it meets the Richmond Turnpike, a hamlet developed around the Bull's Head Tavern, while another of about twenty-five houses cropped up near Springville. Finally, near the hilly geographic center of the north shore, the town of Centerville boasted numerous farms and orchards just west of Silver Lake.[115]

Along with numerous homes, taverns popped up all over Richmond County. There were seaside venues like Purdy's at Prince's Bay and the Dock Hotel at New Brighton, while the St. Mark's Hotel occupied the heights nearby. West Brighton had several, including the Swan Hotel, the Fountain House and the Castleton House on Broadway, which served as the headquarters of the Island's militia unit, the Tompkin's Guards. Port Richmond claimed the aptly named Port Richmond Hotel, where Burr died, as well as Bennett's Tavern and the Northfield Hotel. New Dorp had the Black Horse Tavern and the Patten House, while Oakwood had the Old Track House and the Old Club House, both built in 1828. The town of Richmond boasted the Union Hotel and the Washington Hotel, then affectionately called "Curry's." Farther south, one could find Oakley's Tavern in Rossville and both the Union Hotel and the Ferry Tavern in Tottenville. The two largest and most opulent halls were Nautilus Hall, built in 1808 at Tompkinsville and host to numerous events, and Pavilion Hall, boasting a six-thousand-square-foot saloon under a grand dome supported by an arcade of Corinthian columns.[116]

As its popularity and productivity grew, eighteenth-century Staten Island had a need to transport waves of newcomers to its shorefront and among its villages. Answering this call was one of the county's most prominent and wealthy residents, a man whose family had resided on its shores since the 1715 purchase of several acres by his ancestor, Jacob Van Der Bilt. One of Jacob's great-grandchildren, born into a family of hardscrabble farmers, would change the United States forever and amass one of the largest fortunes on earth.[117]

Cornelius Vanderbilt was born on May 27, 1794, and spent his childhood in a home along the Stapleton shorefront, now the site of the dilapidated Paramount Theater at 560 Bay Street.[118] Most modern accounts place his birthplace elsewhere, and in his own reminiscing, he claimed it was on Port Richmond Avenue, near the location of the Northfield Hotel by Castleton Avenue, where he also met his wife, Sophie.[119]

Cornelius's father would often make morning runs on his boat between Stapleton and New York, ferrying passengers and farm products; by the time he turned eleven, he had skipped school and was manning the vessel himself. He fell in love with the sea, but his parents would not allow him to ship out on a large vessel. In a compromise, his mother helped him scrape together $100 to purchase a periauger, a flat-bottomed boat with two small masts. His original fare to the city was eighteen cents, and with sixteen hours per day, he was able to make $1,000 in his first year.[120] At twenty-three, he progressed into steamboats and was soon commanding an empire around the harbor. He resided at various times on Staten Island in Stapleton and was buried at the Moravian Cemetery in 1877.

Vanderbilt also influenced the development of the county's first rail line. He chose the site of his ferry landing as its northern terminus to sync service. At the opposite end, Totten's Landing was the clear choice. However, there was a significant debate over whose land the thirteen-mile journey would take. The first public meeting was held on August 2, 1851, in Richmond town, at which the railroad was incorporated. Its officers were Joseph Seguine, president; Stephen Seguine, treasurer; and George White, secretary.[121]

Their main challenge was not financial; there seems to have been no problem raising $300,000. However, four years of complications from failed purchases of several rights of way from dozens of property owners forced the company to use the state legislature for acquisitions.[122] At noon on June 2, 1860, the Staten Island Railroad formally opened, with the county's leading citizens and guests from New York making the "delightful trip" south from Vanderbilt's landing.[123]

Unlike the railroad, not all of the county's companies were successful. In 1838, Staten Island's first bank was chartered and christened as the Richmond County Bank.[124] A similar list of prominent men made up the board of trustees, including town supervisors, and many were also coincidentally members of a related public company, the Staten Island Whaling Company.[125]

Many Staten Islanders were outraged over the chartering of a county bank. Banking was a controversial issue in the United States, and the backdrop of Andrew Jackson and the Jacksonian Democrats fighting against the re-authorization of the Bank of the United States in the 1830s and the recession known as the Panic of 1837 provides context. There was also anger against new incorporation laws, which allowed companies to be formed and stocks to be issued without the expressed authorization of the state legislature. Staten Islanders smelled a scam.

The prevailing thought was that a county bank would be "a most flagrant and daring insult to the good sense of the People" and "not sufficient to insure a sound and healthy currency." In addition, there was a concern that the whaling company would, in essence, create a well-funded licensed monopoly for the capturing of whales, preventing future competition. A public meeting to protest both companies was held at the Shakespeare Hotel in Factoryville[126] in 1838, organized by Jacksonian congressman Samuel Barton and former assemblyman Paul Mersereau.[127] The participants adopted resolutions denouncing the enterprises and seeking the legislature's assistance. Although the legislature did not act, the public was clearly dead set against the bank. It went out of business by 1842,[128] and the Whaling Company's factory burned to the ground after the maiden voyage of its only ship, the *White Oak*.[129]

Politics, Parties and Problems

Before Barton and Mersereau's public rally against the bank, the Democratic-Republican Party had trouble establishing a foothold on Staten Island, in spite of the fact that Aaron Burr and Daniel Tompkins were historically two of its most prominent leaders. It wasn't until the factories started opening, steam ferries ended its isolation and the population boomed that Federalist-aligned politicians lost their grip.

In the early nineteenth century, Richmond's voters were slow to warm up to Democratic politicians. Until then, Federalists found votes among a number of different classes who formed their natural base. These included merchants who were fearful of the type of Jacobinism that recently engulfed France; loyalists and their descendants who preferred the United States' relationship with Britain;[130] and the Episcopalian majority who shaped a type of "Anglo-Federal" alliance.[131] Even as other parts of the country bent sharply toward the Jeffersonian party in the lead up to the War of 1812, Staten Island continued to elect Federalists.[132] When the Island finally gave its first Democratic-Republican majority to the George Clinton Jr. in 1806, the vote was almost evenly split.[133]

Between 1800 and 1850, Richmond County's population grew threefold, from 4,564 to 15,061. Another 10,000 came over the next ten years as more and more sought employment in the county's factories and relief from the crowded streets of New York City.[134] To those born and raised on its shores, most of whom at that point could trace their family history to its colonial settlers, these newcomers were termed "outsiders" and treated like interlopers in an insular community. They changed the landscape, the culture and, to a great degree, the political slant of the county electorate. With them came a fresh newspaper in 1831, the *Richmond Republican*, which helped fan the flames of the Democratic Party. Political campaigns were also fundamentally changed and conducted with more vigor than ever. "Calling opponents by hard names seems to have been considered an excellent argument."[135]

Still, the political change was slow. When Paul Mersereau beat his cousin Jacob Mersereau for Assembly in 1833, the vote count stood at 568 to 524 for his Whig opponent. This mimicked other results throughout that decade. In 1837, the Whig Israel Oakley beat Democratic-Republican John Garretson Jr. by 13 for Assembly, while the Democrat Andrew Decker won the sheriff seat by just 10 votes.[136]

In the 1840s, many wealthy New Yorkers began taking up residence and changing the face of local politics. Like today, many found solace on the

Island's tree-lined hilltops, far removed from Manhattan's bustle. Grymes Hill was the most popular destination.

The 374-foot hill was named after Suzette Grymes, the widow of a Louisiana governor who remarried John Randolph Grymes.[137] Their estate, Capo di Monte, was situated on the rise above Broad Street. Soon other grand homes followed. A New York lawyer named John Anthon built an estate called Aquehonga just across the street from his neighbor, Major George Howard. It's now the site of Notre Dame Academy. Down the road, the Nesbith family resided at Inwood, a cluster of homes on the peak just south of modern St. John's University. Next door was Captain Jacob Vanderbilt, the Commodore's brother, followed by the Nichols family's Vale Snowden, designed by renowned architect Fredrick Law Olmsted (who had himself purchased a farm on the Island in Annadale called Akerly Farm). On Grymes Hill's southern tip, Sir Edward Cunard, the 2nd Baronet Cunard and the New York agent of the shipping line, built his Belleview estate in 1853. It's now Wagner College's Cunard Hall.[138]

Just before the outbreak of the Civil War, political tensions were high in Richmond County, and it is somewhat unsurprising that the Island sought to further politically subdivide, albeit peacefully. Since colonial times, Staten Island had been divided into four townships, but on April 16, 1860, the town of Middletown was formed[139] from combined cuts of land from Castleton and Southfield. It encompassed the waterfront from Tompkinsville to the fort and covered the wealthy estates of Grymes, Emerson and Todt Hills.

However, in the months leading up to its formation, it was not entirely clear why the legislature would want to incorporate a new township in the first place. As the *Richmond County Gazette* opined, "We do not see the need for any new towns."[140]

As it turns out, the rationale for forming a fifth township in the otherwise small county had little to do with governance and everything to do with politics. By 1860, the abolition movement and its de facto political arm, the Republican Party, had begun to take hold in New York and much of the North. As it would prove to be at many points in political history, Richmond County was a battleground and slow to change direction with the prevailing political winds. While the state handily voted for Lincoln that year, the Island was one of a small minority of counties to narrowly vote against him.[141]

The fledgling Republican Party was organizing, and one tactic it adopted after overwhelming wins in the state legislature in 1859 was to use its majority to form new Republican-controlled townships. It remains unclear, however, why the county's one assemblyman, Democrat Theodore Vermilye, would not oppose a measure that would surely lead to a new "Republican stronghold" on Staten Island. The *Gazette* claimed, "There would not be a more Conservative town in the County" and called the proposal a "deception," a "scheme so barefaced" and the work of one of Albany's "celebrated lobbymen."[142] Yet despite all of this, and perhaps the real reason Vermilye declined to oppose the bill, Democrats truly believed that they would win a majority of votes. In the end, a staunchly Anti-Lincoln Democrat, Jacob B. Wood, was elected Middletown's first supervisor.[143]

Outside of the traditional partisan battles, this period of Staten Island's history also brought to the forefront a jurisdictional fight that continued to have implications for ferry operations between New York and New Jersey. It would also finally put to rest the question that informally lingered since the legend of Christopher Billop's twenty-four-hour sail around Staten Island: whether Staten Island was legally a part of New York or not.

In the 1824 landmark case of *Gibbons v. Ogden*, which challenged New York's monopoly over coastal shipping, the Supreme Court limited the state's power to regulate interstate commerce. The resolution of this case ended New York's domination of the bay by invalidating some its interstate ferry regulations, but it also placed new pressure on New Jersey to settle its boundary disputes. Based on its colonial patents, New York still claimed ownership and jurisdiction of all of the Hudson and New York Harbor up to the high-water mark of New Jersey, as well as much of its important underwater oyster beds.[144] If these claims could be validated, New York would still maintain control over the harbor, in spite of the Supreme Court's decision.

Staten Island was an active base for enforcing New York's maritime sovereignty. A deputy sheriff of Richmond County was jailed in Middlesex in 1826 after arresting a steamship captain in the shallows off Perth Amboy for unloading passengers against New York law.[145] First, New Jersey appealed to Congress, which refused to intervene. Then its attorney general, Theodore Frelinghuysen, brought another action to the Supreme Court, but it was rebuffed as well. New York offered a token concession: its legislature voted to pull back its border to New Jersey's low-water mark along the Hudson, in Raritan Bay and around Staten Island.[146] This, too, was rejected, but it eventually led Chief Judge Marshall to agree to hear New Jersey's plea despite his reservations that a strong opinion against New York could trigger a second nullification crisis if it did not recognize the court's jurisdiction under the Constitution[147] (the first being the nullification crisis of South Carolina over tariffs only a year earlier).

The court ordered the formation of a bi-state commission, which met in Hoboken in 1833. The resolution set the boundary at the midpoint of the Hudson, as well as that of Raritan Bay, the Arthur Kill and the Kill van Kull. New York was to retain the smaller islands in the harbor and have jurisdiction over passengers traveling over New York Bay; most significant for the future of Staten Island, it would also control the quarantine laws and set policy over all passengers entering the harbor.[148]

THE QUARANTINE, CHOLERA AND CALAMITY

The idea of quarantining sick passengers entering New York Harbor on Staten Island goes back almost as far as the republic itself, to 1799, when the state legislature used eminent domain to acquire thirty acres from St. Andrew's Church on the north shore. Although sparse, the population of the county along with its representative in the Assembly opposed this site, roughly where the present Staten Island Ferry Terminal is. Still, dormitory and medical buildings were thrown up within a year and the first patients disembarked. Sadly, the worst fears soon were realized, as twenty-five cases of yellow fever occurred outside quarantine walls during its first year of operation,[149] resulting in twenty-four deaths.[150]

For the next half century, the quarantine would be a chief source of resentment and concern for Islanders and, sadly, would prove to be only the first time the more powerful city government and state legislature would place unwanted, albeit necessary, facilities in the county. These would later include the Farm Colony for the destitute in the late nineteenth century, as well as the Tuberculosis Sanatorium at Seaview and the city's Fresh Kills Landfill later on. Concern over the quarantine and resulting health scares superseded all other calamities during the first half of the nineteenth century. There were murder trials, heinous scandals and three earthquakes. Still, nothing brought the sensational headlines that accompanied the numerous fights over the quarantine.[151]

From 1800 to 1855, the population of Manhattan rose tenfold to 630,000 as immigrants poured in from Europe on cramped and unsanitary vessels. Before disembarking, they made an obligatory stop at the quarantine, a scene which Thoreau described in 1843:

Sixteen hundred immigrants arrived at quarantine ground on the 4th of July, and more or less every day since I have been here. I see them occasionally washing their persons and clothes: or men, women, and children gathered on an isolated quay near the shore, stretching their limbs and taking the air; the children running races and swinging on this artificial piece of the land of liberty, while the vessels are undergoing purification. They are detained but a day or two, and then go up to the city, for the most part without having landed *here.*[152]

In the same period, Richmond County's population also swelled to twenty-one thousand. While the influx of new citizens in the city pressured authorities to expand capacity of the quarantine, just outside its walls, the surrounding neighborhoods saw more houses as the north shore became densely peopled. Unsurprisingly, death and disease followed.[153]

Yellow fever broke out inside the quarantine in 1821. Within a year, it had spread across Staten Island and caused an epidemic in New York City,[154] killing 3,026. In 1832, it returned, taking 4,882 New Yorkers. In 1832 and 1834, cholera broke out, killing 10,000 citizens each year. Political pressure on the government and a general outrage reached a boiling point when

A view of the quarantine station from Upper New York Bay, painted and engraved in 1833. *Courtesy of the Library of Congress.*

the diseases took 14,882 in 1848.[155] On Staten Island, 180 died as a result of what a panel of inquiry called "corrupt or reckless mismanagement" at the facility.[156]

Finally, the legislature took action. It empaneled a commission to examine the fitness of the site and to make recommendations for its improvement or relocation. Its 1849 findings were unanimous, claiming that the site was "injurious to the health and fatal to the prosperity of Staten Island." It recommended its closure. Still, almost at the same time the report was published, another yellow fever epidemic broke out on Staten Island and "raged with unprecedented violence."[157] It spread to neighboring cities, and in total, 22,605 people died. The legislature simply had to act more decisively.

On April 10, 1849, it passed the "Act for the Establishment of Hospitals at Sandy Hook" and provided it funding and personnel. New York's shipping interests balked. The distance to Sandy Hook would add time and cost; to appease them, the legislation was never carried into effect.[158]

The government failures did nothing to stop the diseases from returning. In 1854, the year the port saw its highest number of immigrants enter the United States, it also saw the highest number of deaths on record, mostly from cholera. In 1856, yellow fever returned and took its toll as well. Once again, Staten Islanders petitioned the legislature to move the quarantine to New Jersey. The results were the same.[159]

The quarantine was also suffering through its worst period of mismanagement. City newspapers ran daily stories of how "promiscuous intercourse was permitted between those inside and outside the walls." In the hot summer of 1856, for example, a group of quarantined stevedores left the premises for a political meeting in New Brighton, where just days later multiple cases of yellow fever broke out. In response, Staten Island's county and town leaders got more extreme as more of their citizens became ill. The board of health of the town of Castleton went as far as erecting its own barriers outside of the quarantine. But soon a mob of angry quarantine patients emerged to tear it down.[160]

The next year, the commissioners of emigration addressed the problem in a way that incited even more Staten Islanders. Instead of removing the quarantine from the county, they purchased the farm of Joel Wolfe in a comparatively remote part of the south shore, just east of Seguine's Point. Residents were outraged, as the *New York Herald* reported, "This hostility pervades all classes, from the wealthy gentlemen who occupy summer villas on the Island, to the humblest oysterman who works for his dollar a day."[161]

Almost as soon as construction began, hooligans burned down one of its outlying buildings, causing the city to send a detachment of the Metropolitan Police to stand guard. On the night of July 11, 1857, twenty-five officers were asleep in a bunkhouse while two stood watch. At 11:00 p.m., a "gang of about 150 of the disaffected inhabitants residing in the vicinity of Seguine's Point"[162] made its move. Thirty armed men approached from the south and attacked the police, while another group attacked the dock builders bunking just to the north. The sergeant in charge fired a warning shot from his musket; an instant later, the attackers fired back, striking him in the hand. The mob took positions behind the ruins of the burned-out building and kept a continuous fire on the bunkhouse, while the other group began shooting from the rear. The distance between each group was more than five hundred yards, and the musket fire was inaccurate. After about ten minutes of fighting, the result was nothing more than a few flesh wounds, and in the end, the police were able to repel the attack.[163] They were forced to keep a large garrison at Seguine's Point and at the quarantine for the next several months, as threats of violence persisted.[164]

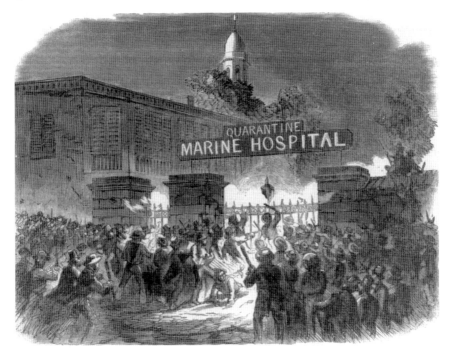

An engraving published in *Harper's Weekly* depicting the violent raid on the quarantine station on September 1, 1858. *Courtesy of the Library of Congress.*

The following summer, the situation escalated. A ship, the *Rattler*, saw several cases of yellow fever on its way from New Orleans and entered New York Harbor. Two passengers had already died, and two dockworkers soon fell ill as they reloaded the ship with cargo.[165] The mayor was incensed and threatened to scuttle the ship at its slip if it was not immediately moved out of the city. It was brought to a dock in Tompkinsville, near the original Quarantine, and soon after the Castleton Board of Health reported twenty-six cases and ten deaths among its residents.[166]

Again the board denounced the quarantine, but this time it went as far as urging the citizens of the county to abate the problem. A mob assembled atop Fort Hill at around 9:00 p.m. on September 1, 1858, and after publicly reading the report of the Castleton Board of Health, they armed themselves with turpentine, straw and matches and set off down the hill. Conveniently, or intentionally, some of the gates in the quarantine's brick walls were left open, and they were able to easily enter, despite a few shots fired from the officers.[167]

The mob, reportedly consisting of four hundred people, "removed the patients from the various wards and placed them in open air at about a

This page and opposite: A collection of images depicting the quarantine on Hoffman Island, showing the conditions in which condemned immigrants were held and the dining hall where they were fed. *Courtesy of the Library of Congress.*

hundred yards distance, and proceeded with their destruction." They lit the mattresses to assist burning the hospitals and moved on to the other buildings. After two men were hit by gunfire and two brick hospitals, five dorms, the "dead house," the doctor's residence, stables and outhouses were burned to rubble, the gang retired.[168]

Still, it was not over. Fueled by rumors that the army would arrive to rebuild, the mob gathered the following day at Nautilus Hall. Led by Ray Tompkins, they marched down to the quarantine and burned all of the remaining structures still standing.[169] On the third day, one hundred policemen were brought in to restore order, armed with "volcanic repeating rifles and pistols" and one six-pounder for good measure. Tents were pitched within the rubble walls of the quarantine for both the displaced patients and the officers on guard duty. The *Evening Post* dubbed the incident the "Quarantine War" and compared the scene to the "encampment of the allied armies within the ruins of Sebastopol."[170]

Soon the walls were rebuilt and the site garrisoned by militia companies. The area around the quarantine was placed under martial law for several months, and legal action was taken against Ray Tompkins and another instigator, John Thompson. The county was forced to pay for the damages.

However, the "Quarantine War" was a victory for Staten Island. Between 1859 and 1863, sick patients were temporarily housed on two floating hospital ships, *Falcon* and *Florence Nightingale*, and those who died were buried at Seguine's Point, likely on the city-owned property bought from Wolfe. (The bodies were removed and incinerated around 1890.) Two manmade barrier islands were constructed just offshore from South Beach, and the quarantine operations were completed on them for more than fifty years. The buildings on Hoffman (Upper Quarantine) Island and Swinburne (Lower Quarantine) Island have since been razed, but the islands are still visible from shore and are protected as bird sanctuaries.[171]

CHAPTER 2

"Richmond Co. Arouse!"

Unlike the Revolution, the horrors of combat did not visit Staten Island during the Civil War. Yet for certain the war had an indelible impact on the county's 25,507 people, of which 4,888 were men between fifteen and forty years old.[172] Thousands would serve. Many would die.

The Island itself would be swept up and transformed in the war effort, as coastal defenses around New York Bay, including those at the Narrows, would be beefed up in an effort to prevent any attacks. Richmond's fields would be turned into mass encampments and training grounds for countless units on their way to the front, and despite serving on the same side, a great many of these troops would prove problematic for the local populace.

Staten Island would not be spared from the political turmoil of the war years. Anger would boil over, and mobs roamed the streets. The Draft Riots of 1863, spreading from Manhattan, echoed loudly on its shores, where gunfire was also used to silence the crowds. The county's 659 "free coloreds"[173] were not always safe, even on this sparsely populated islet a hundred miles north of the Mason-Dixon line and where the abolition movement was a noticeable force.

In the two centuries of European settlement, Staten Island, like most other places in the United States, witnessed a wide spectrum of beliefs and practices regarding slavery, ranging from its participation in the slave trade to its abolitionist fervor. No discussion of the Civil War could be complete without discussing this history in the county, as well as the prevailing beliefs of many residents at the outset of the conflict.

Slavery on Staten Island

The practice of slavery likely existed on Staten Island as far back as the first Dutch attempts to settle its hills. Slaves were in New Amsterdam servicing the West India Company since the 1620s. Although the company chose not to rely solely on slave labor, enough had been brought into the colony to force the construction of their own segregated quarters on Roosevelt Island by 1639.[174]

The earliest record of African American slavery in Richmond County from the census of 1698, when 76 Blacks were listed.[175] Over the next hundred years, their number would grew to nearly 900, peaking at 23 percent of the population. About 125 were freemen.[176]

Dutch and English views on slavery varied in the eighteenth century, but what is clear is that it was more common to find slaves in areas that were settled by Dutch farmers. In contemporary descriptions, travelers were known to report on the prevalence of slaves working the fields of even the poorest Dutch farmers. Census data backs this up, as 28 percent of Dutch households in New York State listed at least one slave, as compared to just 11 percent of English households. The Dutch rate of slave ownership was surpassed only by settlers from France, who by then also made up a significant part of Staten Island's inhabitants.[177] Despite the lower prevalence, it was, however, documented that English slave owners were known to treat their slaves with much less kindness and granted fewer privileges than the Dutch.[178]

The colonial records indicate that the provincial pattern was mimicked to a large extent on Staten Island. In 1755, for example, most of the names listed as owners in a "Census of Slaves" appear to be of Dutch or French descent, owning on average two or three slaves. The Dongan family was the exception, being English and having a comparatively larger total of ten slaves.[179]

The records were quite specific. Thomas Dongan owned Thomas Tice, Jack Mollato, Joe, Phillis and Hanna, among others; while the Corsens claimed a Jupeter, Mary and Rose. Bastian Ellis owned Tom. The 1755 register lists fifty-five slaves in total in the "North Company" of Staten Island but makes no mention of their age, marital status or offspring. Their lives are summed typically in four words. For example, "1 Negro na[med] Tom" was written underneath that of their master, "Barnit De Pue."[180]

Unlike its southern counterparts, late eighteenth-century slavery in the North, and specifically on Staten Island, was a more intimate affair. Instead of great plantations with dedicated quarters, slaves of both sexes would often sleep in their master's kitchen. In winter, everyone was likely to be huddled around the same large fire as they ate and slept. Enslaved men would normally work in the fields alongside the white men, while the women performed household duties inside. At night, it was common for Black women to spin linen or twine, while the men would spin heavier yarn that could be sold to rope makers.[181]

In the 1790s, views on slavery began to change in New York State, and as the population of the frontier counties grew, the hegemony of elected officials from the Dutch-heavy Hudson Valley and New York Harbor area dissipated. In 1799, the legislature passed the Gradual Manumissions Act, which freed all new children born to slaves from then on. Still, many families kept up the practice, and by 1810 Kings, Queens and Richmond Counties had the highest rates of slave ownership in the state, with nearly one out of every five households owning at least one.[182] The Perine family, the occupants of the Billiou-Stillwell-Perine House in the early nineteenth century, purchased "One Certain Negro Boy, named France" in March 1801 for $175.[183] The Perines likely thought that the seventeen-year-old boy could work for them for several decades to come.

New Jersey was slower in adapting its views on slavery, and Staten Islanders may have taken advantage of that. At the end of the eighteenth century and beginning of the nineteenth century, the city of Amboy, which shared Raritan Bay with the thriving Staten Island oyster industry on the south shore, was a major port and market for the slave trade and provided human cargo for places as far away as Louisiana.[184] The port of Amboy had long served as a destination for slave traders wishing to avoid the laws and custom duties of New York, since at least the first instance in 1683,[185] and it is reasonable to surmise that some ended up in their neighboring province and state. Their slave market was so lucrative that on the eve of the Revolution, the citizens of Amboy petitioned their colonial government to withdraw support for a bill that would simplify the process of voluntary manumission on the grounds that it would complicate the thriving trade in their city.[186]

Still, the impact of the Gradual Manumissions Act began to become evident, and documentation of this survives as excerpts from the town records reprinted in *Morris's Memorial History of Staten Island*. After the law was enacted, a log called a "Town Book" was kept and certified by the town clerk of all African American births to ensure their freedom and county's compliance with the act.[187] For example, on page twenty-four of the Town Book for Castleton (which was given to the New York Historical Society by

Ira Morris in 1901 and is now digitized), James Guyon records the births of a Mary (1814) and Harry (1817) to his "Woman of Colour," named Mary, and a third baby named Murry (1816) to a different slave, listed as Jane.[188] Many Staten Island slave owners went beyond what was required by law and manumitted other Black children prior to the expiration of the period they were required to work; still others began freeing many adults.[189] For example, one order signed by Judge David Mersereau reads, "I do hereby certify that Henry Byers a Black Person is free according to the Laws of this State and That he is twenty two years of age & that he…obtained his freedom on the 24th day of April 1811."[190]

These Town Books give an idea of which prominent families were still owning slaves in the nineteenth century. In Castleton, the Garretsons and Corsens are on the list; while in Northfield, the list includes Cornelius Bedell, John Crocheron and John Tysen. In Southfield, where the records were sparse, the names include Tottens, Journeys, Morgans and a Barnes. At the time, Westfield was the wealthiest town in the county and had the most slaves. There, the slave owning families encompassed the Tottens, Winants, Van Dykes, Seguines, Androvettes, Dissosways, Butlers, Latourettes and many others.[191]

Despite its prevalence on Staten Island, slavery was on its way out in New York. In 1808, the legislature increased the penalty against kidnapping slaves, and two years later, the importation of slaves by any New York State resident was outlawed. The most important change came in 1817 with the passage of another manumission act under Governor Tompkins, effectively emancipating every slave in the state in ten years' time.[192]

On July 4, 1827, this act went into effect with great fanfare on Staten Island, including an official celebration at the Swan Hotel in New Brighton, where "scores of old masters mingled in the crowds of happy negroes."[193] At the time of emancipation, there were 692 slaves, and nearly every man, woman and child took part in the festivities, which included speeches from both Democrats and Whigs, as well as the county's most prominent Black citizens. Among the speakers were the Island's member of the State Assembly, Hermanus Garrison; Judge Jacob Tysen; County Clerk Jonathan Lewis; Surrogate Judge Tunis Egbert; Sheriff Walter Betts; District Attorney Henry Metcalfe; and the four town supervisors, Isaac Housman of Castleton, Nicholas Crocheron of Northfield, Harmanus Guyon of Southfield and Gilbert Totten of Westfield.[194]

After the success in New York, many Staten Islanders were eager to take part in the broader national abolition movement. More significantly, the county itself became a magnet for former slaves from around New York, New Jersey and beyond.

In 1828, a free black ferryboat captain named John Jackson purchased land just south of Rossville, in an area known as Sandy Ground. For nearly two hundred years, this settlement has the distinction of being the longest continually occupied settlement of former slaves, and many of the descendants of the original families still live in the neighborhood.[195]

Soon after Jackson, the Harris brothers bought land and began farming strawberries in the sandy soil. Within a few years, they had amassed a net worth of about $6,000, a sum essentially making them gentleman farmers.[196] In the 1840s and 1850s, the population of the community swelled and grew to about fifty houses, as an influx of migration came from the South. The State of Maryland had passed a series of harsh and oppressive laws against free blacks; in response, many oystermen then living in Snow Hill, and elsewhere along the Chesapeake Bay, moved to Sandy Ground to take advantage of the liberal laws and Staten Island's rich oyster beds.[197]

At Sandy Ground, the growing African American community was able to own property and grow with the prosperity that Staten Island at large saw in the mid-1800s. Soon, like the rest of the county, it was erecting its own institutions. Its heyday came after the war, during Reconstruction, when, as sociologist William Askins claimed, the community achieved both "economic success and a recognition of relative equality in their residential community."[198] The community was made up of both Black and white residents (in 1900, the census shows about half of the residents of Sandy Ground as white),[199] and its school, run by Esther Purnell, was responsible for educating Westfield's students of all races. In 1849, Reverend William H. Pitts, a Virginia-born African Methodist Episcopal Zion minister, purchased land on Crabtree Avenue and held home prayer services for the town. By 1854, the congregation had built its own church and was large enough to accommodate 150 worshipers.[200] (This is not the structure that still stands at 584 Bloomingdale Road.) On nearby land, they founded the Sandy Ground Cemetery, now a designated landmark and the site of nearly all of the community's notable burials, including Captain Johnson.[201] In 2016, a study using ground-penetrating radar discovered more than five hundred additional unmarked graves.[202]

One of those burials, or perhaps lying in a still-unknown grave near his home at 570 Bloomingdale Road, likely contains the remains of one of Sandy Ground's most notable residents, the abolitionist Louis Napoleon. As early as the 1840s, there is evidence that he served along the Underground

Railroad; by war's end, he had likely helped more than three thousand self-emancipators find freedom. His work was so well known that at the time of his passing, the occupation attributed to him on his death certificate was "Underground R.R. Agent."[203] Staten Island was a significant stop along two routes of the Underground Railroad, with passengers crossing the kill either at Perth Amboy or Elizabeth. The passage was dangerous, as schooners operating in the waters during the 1850s were often searched for fugitive slaves in violation of Virginia's broad inspection laws. This continued right up to the outbreak of the war.[204]

THE POLITICS OF WAR

The question of slavery incited the same emotions on Staten Island as it did elsewhere in the United States in the lead up to the Civil War. However, Richmond County and others surrounding New York City also faced controversial questions over immigration, with both issues making their way to the forefront of newspaper headlines and popular political discourse.

By 1850, the two parties that held near-hegemony over the body politic of the country each began to disintegrate in its own way. The Democrats, who reached a pinnacle under the era of Andrew Jackson, eroded over third-party involvement and internal disputes over patronage, while their opposition, the Whigs, suffered an outright collapse.[205]

The Whigs split into two factions. One was solidly against slavery, emerging as the Republican Party in 1854; the other tolerated it, in addition to supporting nativism, xenophobia and anti-Catholicism. The latter became the "Know Nothings" in 1854 because when asked about their membership and beliefs, they would typically respond that they "know nothing." New York, with its tradition of abolition and two-century history of immigration, was front and center in the scrap between the former Whig adherents. In the state, the Republican Party was led by U.S. Senator William Seward, later to serve as Lincoln's secretary of state; his archrival, former president Millard Fillmore, carried the banner for the Know Nothings.[206]

On Staten Island, elections in the 1850s certainly underscored the divide and showed the depth of competing views on slavery and immigrants. At that time, and much like today, New York City and its surrounding counties were home to more foreign-born citizens than anywhere else in the country. The booming factories on Staten Island were the final destination of many new migrants from Europe, and those who came were predominately Irish

Catholic, although some were German. The latter organized their first religious congregation around this time, the German Evangelical Lutheran Church of St. John, and in 1852, it purchased its church on Jewett Avenue from a Methodist congregation.[207]

The Irish Catholic rate of immigration was exponentially higher. St. Peter's Church in New Brighton was first organized in 1839, although the number of its congregants was so few that its first pastor, a Spaniard named Father Ildefenso Medrano, shared his time with congregations in Perth Amboy and New Brunswick. In one decade, the population grew so quickly that a second parish was needed at Rossville, called St. Joseph's; the Island did still manage with one priest, then Father Patrick Murphy. The young priest had the additional duty of ministering to the Catholic immigrants at the quarantine, and sadly, his work with the sick caused his death from yellow fever in 1848.[208]

As anti-Catholicism and nativism grew, rooting itself in local politics, even more Catholic immigrants found homes on Staten Island. By the outbreak of war, two more parishes had been formed: St. Mary's in Rosebank and St. Patrick's in Richmond;[209] in 1860, there were 8,563 Roman Catholics on Staten Island. Seemingly overnight, they grew to more than one-third of the population.[210]

Immigrants altered the demographics of Staten Island, and changing political sentiments played out in the growing number of competing newspapers. Prior to 1827, the county did not have any of its own, a fact that changed with the establishment of the *Richmond Republican*. In the 1830s, it was owned by William Hagadorn, effectively the first newspaper magnate of the Island. It had a decidedly Democratic bias and didn't hide its support of President Jackson.[211]

Hagadorn and his son started several other smaller papers over the next two decades. Most notably, the *Semi-Weekly Staten Islander* opened its doors in 1856 and gave a strong voice to those with racially conservative views and southern sympathies. It was politically allied with the Democratic Party and its presidential nominee, James Buchanan.[212]

Despite Buchanan's eventual win, Hagadorn was up against a growing tide of abolitionist fervor. Instead of seeking to win the hearts and minds of those families who had been here for generations, the paper was targeted at drumming up resentment among the new Irish and German populations. In this, he was successful. Hundreds of Germans shunned the Republican nominee and joined in the ranks of the Democratic Party of Richmond County.[213]

George William Curtis, one of the most prominent Staten Islanders in the nineteenth century, was a leading abolitionist and involved in the founding of the Republican Party. *Courtesy of the New York Public Library.*

When the election came, Staten Island's voters mimicked the national trend. The split in the former Whig Party threw the county for Buchanan, despite the Democrats only taking 47 percent of the vote. Buchanan trounced the competition at polling sites on the north shore, including Factoryville and Tompkinsville, which had outsized immigrant populations. At Clifton, then known as Vanderbilt's Landing, its poll site saw the largest crowds of the day, and violence broke out between Democrats and their rivals. If the issue of slavery did not divide the Republicans and Know Nothings, they would have won the majority.[214]

One of the other results of the election of 1856 was the further organization of the abolition movement on Staten Island; in a significant way, the county was intrinsically tied to the start of the Republican Party by some of those same notable people. John C. Frémont, the party's first candidate for president, lived for a time on Staten Island at the corner of Bay Street and Simonson Avenue (now Townsend Avenue[215]), and it's rumored that he received the news of his defeat there. One early twentieth-century tourist guide to the Island even went as far as naming the Island as the "First National Headquarters of the Republican Party,"[216] although most of the work during the election took place in New York City. Still, it earned that moniker due to the work of prominent abolitionists like Frémont, as well as Sidney Howard Gay, Francis George Shaw and George William Curtis.[217]

Gradually, the clique of abolitionists grew, and their work became more noticeable. One writer described the scene: "Propaganda at all times was in order, lectures, and meetings continually, and once a year a great Anti-Slavery Fair."[218] The cause was faithfully espoused by the "Black Republicans," as they were derided by their opponents, for four years straight through to the next election in 1860. In conjunction with an organization they formed called the North Shore Lecture Committee, what started out as small lectures soon became lyceum-style public gatherings. In 1859, notable abolitionists like Horace Greeley and Wendell Phillips were soon on the speakers list, often giving orations to hundreds of Islanders.[219]

John C. Frémont—officer, expeditionary and U.S. senator—was the first Republican nominee for president in 1856, while residing on Staten Island and collaborating with local abolitionists. *Courtesy of the Library of Congress.*

On the other side, however, the proslavery and pro–Democratic Party reaction was just as strong. On November 4, the scheduled night of Phillips's speech, a small but unfriendly mob gathered outside the Park Avenue Baptist Church in Port Richmond. As a precaution, George Curtis had pre-positioned a band of roughly twenty armed abolitionists to protect the audience while he spoke. They proved their worth, and instead of executing a plan to kidnap Phillips and leave him for dead in the West Shore salt marshes, the mob had to settle on harassing those who exited the church.[220]

The next year, Curtis established the Richmond County Republican Party, which held its first two meetings in August for the purpose of organizing support around their presidential candidate, Abraham Lincoln. The first, on August 1, 1860, took place at the Bull's Head House, with the second at the New Brighton Assembly Rooms. Both featured speeches from Curtis himself, as well as Minthorne Tompkins, who had previously served in the Senate and Assembly as a Jacksonian Democrat.[221]

Joining abolitionists in this new Republican alliance was another organization eager to make its presence known on the Island. Called the "Wide Awakes," this group "donned uniforms, lit torches, and 'fell-in' to pseudo-military marching companies"[222] to demonstrate their support for Lincoln in every town. In total, hundreds of thousands of members swelled the ranks of this grassroots movement.[223] As the *New York Herald* put it, "The greatest feature of the campaign of 1860 has been the introduction of a vast republican auxiliary, semi-military in its character, political in its purpose, and daily increasing in strength and influence to an extent unparalleled in the political annals of our country."[224]

Tensions were already high on September 26, when Republicans gathered at the Jones' Hotel in Tompkinsville for the "largest political assemblage ever gathered together on the Island," where the Wide Awakes "were in very numerous attendance, and gave great animation to the occasion."[225] However, the fervor for Lincoln was not unanimous. Even the New York City press noticed this, claiming, "It is said the population of oystermen…have no means to enlighten themselves on the merits of the Republican question, and remain still under the weight of the democratic and American opinions and prejudices."[226] After the meeting, as two companies of Wide Awakes walked past the walls of the quarantine, they came under an assault from "a band of ruffians, who hurled stones and other missiles upon them, and severely cut a number about the head and face besides breaking several lanterns."[227] Soon, they were thwarted by a violent response by Republican partisans. Amazingly, the incident ended without the loss of life.

For the next month, Republicans held meetings throughout the Island: at Richmond, at the Bull's Head House and at the Pagoda Hotel in Clifton. Their Democratic Party counterparts met frequently too. They were led by Assemblyman Erastus Brooks, Joshua Mersereau, Gabriel Disosway and

Erastus Brooks, a journalist by trade, served Staten Island in the State Senate in the 1850s and the State Assembly in the 1870s and '80s and ran unsuccessfully for governor in 1856. *Courtesy of the New York Public Library.*

Colonel Ray Tompkins,[228] who would soon lead the 73rd Infantry Regiment of the state militia.[229] To many on Staten Island, the arguments against Lincoln were fairly straightforward: avoid a war, preserve the union and save the commercial prosperity that the long-standing trade with the planters and pickers of the South had brought to New York Harbor.

The election was held on November 6, 1860. In total, 3,778 Staten Islanders showed up to the polls—half of eligible voters. Lincoln won New York State, but Richmond County joined New York City, Brooklyn and Long Island in delivering margins for the Democratic ticket. In total, just about one-third of Staten Island's electors cast their lot with the Republicans.[230]

The 1860 ballot also held a referendum on a state constitutional amendment that would have offered universal suffrage and rights to all of the state's African American citizens. The Republican view on this proposal fared worse in the county than even their candidates, with just a paltry 145 people casting their ballot in favor of the measure. The overwhelming bulk of Staten Islanders, even a majority of those voting for Lincoln, were not ready for such a progressive approach to Black citizenship.[231]

The apparent sentiment of Staten Island, and almost all "downstaters" as well, was that Lincoln's election to the presidency would bring nothing but problems for an otherwise prosperous region. The feeling was so strong that New York City mayor Fernando Wood proposed that the landmasses of Manhattan Island, Staten Island and Long Island themselves secede from the Union to form the free city of "Tri-Insula." The City Council quickly passed a supporting resolution.[232] It is easy to dismiss the mayor's idea as outlandish, as most contemporary newspapers did; however, it certainly was a culmination of a number of political grievances in the proposed free city against the new Republican Party. Wood and his acolytes on Staten Island and Long Island were particularly perturbed at bills pushed through by Republican governor John King and the state legislature that limited local control on licenses and municipal police control. For Staten Island, it meant that the county would lose its hegemony in granting liquor licenses to Albany bureaucrats, while its police force would be managed by a commission dominated by New York City appointees, proving a source of concern long after the war.[233]

It was only after the secession of South Carolina and the outbreak of war that most downstaters, including Staten Island, began to rally behind Lincoln's battle cry to preserve the Union.[234]

TO ARMS

The descent into war happened rapidly after Lincoln's election. South Carolina seceded on December 20, 1860, and in February, Jefferson Davis was elected president of the Confederate States. On April 12, Fort Sumter was attacked. As this occurred, the Island was rallying its citizenry around the cause and beginning to mobilize for the impending conflict. On January 26, Tottenville was the site of a massive meeting, during which each orator churned up a pro-Lincoln fervor with "the most enthusiastic expressions of loyalty to the country," all under a giant banner that read "The Constitution and the Union." Guns fired a salute for each state of the Union, for General Winfield Scott and for Major Robert Anderson, the commanding officer at Fort Sumter.[235]

On April 15, after the news of the surrender reached his ears, Lincoln put out his first call for seventy-five thousand volunteers to serve three-month enlistments. By then, it seemed that his political enemies had put some of their differences behind them. George Curtis, the leading Republican in the county, organized recruitment meetings and arranged financial provisions for the families of those serving, while it fell to Colonel Tompkins, an outspoken critic of Lincoln's, to piece together Staten Island's first volunteer regiment. Forty-three joined in the first round.[236]

Throughout the year, the Island had no shortage of successful recruitment drives, both for regiments levied directly by the county and those raised by companies incidentally camped on its shores. By the end of November 1861, the town of Castleton alone had sent 128 men into combat regiments. They left behind 64 families who were cared for out of the considerable sum of $3,250, which the townspeople raised collectively.[237]

Recruitment continued well into the following year, reaching a fever pitch in the summer as the federal government called for 600,000 new volunteers. Again, former political adversaries joined together for the common cause. George Curtis and Democrat Erastus Brooks spoke together at public meetings at Factoryville, Southfield, Elm Park, Port Richmond and New Brighton.[238] The drives did not always prove fruitful, and there was a fear that Staten Island wouldn't meet its quota of 788 men. Although 796 men enlisted that year, three of the companies formed under Colonel Tomkins were forced to split up and supplement the 156th Regiment of New York City, which caused fights, stabbings and burned barracks as the troops struggled to mesh with their new unit.[239]

Difficulty in recruiting continued throughout the war, with particularly disastrous and violent results in 1863 with the implementation of the draft. In 1864, it was so difficult to recruit volunteers that Staten Island officials induced men with offers of $400 per person, with $200 going to the soldier and $200 to any broker who procured him. By September, that sum had jumped to a whopping $700.[240]

With the prospect of earning tremendous amounts of money in short order on one end and the immense potential for death and injury at the other, there were numerous cases of corruption for those seeking to avoid serving in the war effort and those seeking to profit from the trafficking of willing volunteers. For those seeking exemptions, once healthy men asserted countless new hardships, illnesses and injuries in official claims to the county surrogate judge, Henry Metcalfe. Not all were fearful of combat, however, instead fearing the loss of their livelihood to immigrants or free blacks should they be gone for months. On the opposite end, the rampant corruption at the recruiting station at Nautilus Hall in New Brighton caused the *Richmond County Gazette* to give it the moniker of the "Swindling Shop," as the majority of the bounties offered ended up in the hands of those employed in the shady business of brokering volunteers.[241]

Hostilities on the Homefront

As in the Revolution and the French and Indian War, Staten Island soon became a hub for staging and encampments due to its situation at the mouth of the busiest harbor in the North. It was also garrisoned, as it was in the War of 1812, to counter possible incursions into the city.

From the start of the conflict to the surrender at Appomattox, it was common to see troops drilling on the Island's abundant cleared fields. The New Dorp beach area alone contained three Union encampments. Camps Vanderbilt, Yates and Lafayette could each house a full regiment,[242] and the very beauty of that neighborhood was an enticement for recruitment officers. One broadside advertisement for the Eleventh Regiment, "now in camp at New Dorp," claimed that it occupied the "most delightful spot on Staten Island," complete with the "best of sea-bathing and fishing."[243]

By 1863, the New Dorp encampments had grown even larger to include a massive facility called Sprague Barracks, described by the *New York Times* as "in all respects superior to any camp yet located there."[244] The camp functioned as a training ground, prison and hospital, and the records from 1863, particularly after Gettysburg and the draft riots, lists dozens of desertions and deaths occurring there.[245]

Another recruitment poster demanded "Richmond Co. Arouse!" and sought "first-class men only" for the "first-rate Richmond Co. Regiment"[246] under Colonel Tompkins. Before its combination with the New York Regiments under Frances Spinola (later the first Italian American elected to Congress), this unit was originally camped at Camp McClellan in Factoryville, between modern Castleton Avenue and Richmond Terrace. In all, a further six camps would be used throughout the war: Camp Leslie in Clifton; Camp Herndon along the Stapleton waterfront; Camp Morrison along St. Paul's Avenue; Camp Scott in Old Town, encompassing the present site of PS 46 and the playground; Camp Low in Elm Park; and Camp Ward in Port Richmond.[247]

Outside of housing and training troops prior to embarkation to the front, Staten Island again played a critical role in the coastal defenses of New York Harbor. After the War of 1812, the federal government approved an $18 million plan to construct "third system fortifications" around the nation's important harbors. Among the fifty sites originally proposed, New York was high on the priority list, and work quickly began improving the works at the Narrows.[248]

At the outbreak of war, there were well over 125 naval guns trained seaward from the system of forts at the Narrows. The main battery at Fort Richmond was reconstructed with its iconic four-tiered design in 1837[249] and had between 140 and 150 guns in total.[250] Additionally, Battery Hudson and Battery Morton were reinforced in 1862, causing the *Richmond County Gazette* to note that the fort was "daily strengthened by all the means and applications of modern warfare" and "garrisoned by quite a stronger force of soldiers from the 5th Regiment N.Y.V. Artillery; Col. Graham, who daily practices with the large guns."[251]

The howitzers of Staten Island never fired in anger, and the Island, like almost all of the North, was spared the ravages of war. The ships that worked

An engraving depicting a Union flotilla attacking Fort Jackson in the Lower Mississippi, including the USS *Westfield*, a converted Staten Island ferry, with its identifiable paddle wheel. *Courtesy of the British Library.*

the county's waters did, however, find their way into the conflict. Historians Richard Bayles and Ira Morris each cite the seizure of the Staten Island schooner *S.W. Lutrell* off the coast of Norfolk in 1861 for violating Virginia's fugitive slave laws in their annals of the county; other chroniclers ignore the incident, however, and there does not seem to be any newspaper reports to back it up.[252] Still, there is certainty that other Staten Island ships were affected, including its ferries. *Clifton* and *Northfield* were retrofitted for combat in 1863, and within months of its purchase from Cornelius Vanderbilt,[253] the *Westfield* was in the Gulf of Mexico participating in the successful Siege of New Orleans and attack on Vicksburg. But on January 1, 1863, it ran aground while under heavy fire from a Confederate flotilla at the Battle of Galveston.[254] Rather than allow *Westfield* to fall into Rebel hands, its Brooklyn-born captain, William Renshaw, scuttled the ship.[255] While ablaze, it prematurely exploded and killed the captain and thirteen crewmen. About 150 years later, portions of the *Westfield* were salvaged and placed on display as part of a U.S. Army Corps of Engineers' project to deepen Galveston's shipping channels.[256]

On the Island, the overwhelming majority of the thousands of Union soldiers who were housed and trained were not native to its shores. From the outset, sporadic problems materialized between enlisted men and the local populace, including the women, whether in and around camp or on leave in the towns.

"Some of 'Wilson's Boys' in wooded camp on Staten Island." A contemporary sketch of Wilson's Zouaves lounging around camp in 1861. *Courtesy of the New York Public Library.*

One of the first units to camp on Staten Island landed at the quarantine grounds on April 24, 1861. The detachment consisted of the first five companies of the 6th New York Volunteers, otherwise known as the "Wilson Zouaves."[257] In the nineteenth century, Zouaves were modeled on French light infantry, often wearing red baggy pantaloons and occasionally a fez. In the case of the 6th, men were often recruited from some of the city's least desirable citizens, including Bowery street gangs,[258] and as Colonel Wilson mustered them at their first meeting at Tammany Hall, they were just as eager to shout "Death to the secessionists!" as they were of their gangland rivals "Death to the Plug Uglies!"[259]

While on Staten Island, they were known to hop the walls of the quarantine and roam through towns, "visiting the houses and annoying the inhabitants." According to Bayles, "Many petty depredations and thefts were committed by them," and several were arrested.[260] Writing just after the war's end, the Zouaves' regimental historian recalled the time in camp slightly different, however, and claimed any of "the current newspaper slurs about the conduct of the Sixth, by the ladies of Staten Island"[261] were unwarranted and overblown.

It is of little surprise that many of the incidents of harassment, crimes and scrapping committed by delinquent troops are linked, at least in the estimation of their commanders, to the consumption of alcohol. One notorious source of liquor was a cottage located just north of Camp Scott in Old Town, likely along Richmond Road, which the soldiers affectionately called "The Canteen." There was more than one complaint of intoxicated men terrorizing the neighborhood and then passing out cold in the nearby woods rather than returning to camp.[262] In 1862, The Canteen itself was actually destroyed by an angry mob of drunken soldiers.[263]

An unidentified soldier wearing a Union Zouave uniform, photographed in Manchester, Rhode Island. *Courtesy of the Library of Congress.*

Writing just twenty years after the war ended, Richard Bayles summarized the problem of disorderly soldiers on Staten Island:

> *The frequent disturbances created by drunken soldiers and the consequent insults and annoyances that the people suffered from them, together with the discord generated by the efforts that were made to suppress liquor selling to the soldiers, and the resistance of a numerous and determined band of liquor dealers who were tempted by the unusual profits to continue in the business all conspired to add more fuel to the flames of popular passion.*
>
> *The petty depredations frequently committed by soldiers encamped here, and the fear of still greater insecurity from that source led to the organization of a "Home Guard," and a volunteer police force, to be called out…in case of any general disturbance that might be caused by the lawlessness of the men from the encampments.*[264]

The use of a corps of Home Guard was less common in the North than in the South, where units were often unpaid, poorly organized and served as a combination of law enforcement and last line of defense. In New York, newspapers reported that Home Guard troops were "drilled in both infantry and artillery work,"[265] and during periods of unrest, some fire companies also "formed themselves into a home guard to protect the property of their neighborhood from the crowd."[266]

According to contemporary accounts, the need to protect residents from the troops was warranted. The Corcoran Legion, for example, consisting of a half dozen regiments of New York City Irish volunteers,[267] was camped for a brief period at Camp Scott. When they departed the Island in November 1862, the *Gazette* asked, "Who is sorry? Not the farmer whose hen roosts were robbed…nor his wife and daughters, who were insulted in broad day and jeered at with foulest language by the ruffian soldiery—not the public officers of the County…who dare not arrest a man of their number unless they run the risk of having daylight let through their unfortunate bodies by bayonet thrusts."[268] It went on to describe "night made hideous by such a collection of barbarians as the Corcoran Legion for the most were. There were good men among them, but they were rare."[269]

In truth, the overwhelming majority of encounters between citizens and soldiers were seldom as sensational as newspaper accounts suggest. Many enjoyed them. Eight thousand spectators lined the grounds of Camp Sprague in September 1863, as General McClellan spoke to and reviewed five infantry and three cavalry regiments on parade.[270] Smaller marches were typically visible to the public on Sundays, and along the camp fences, it was common to see Staten Islanders selling all sorts of fruits, candies and nuts to the eager soldiers, whether they be encamped for training or respite.[271]

STATEN'S SONS

In the earliest campaigns of the war, Staten Island troops played an active role in combat. The initial enlistees were in the mix when the Union suffered its first defeat in 1861. In an article entitled "Our Staten Island Boys at Bull Run," the *Richmond County Gazette* reported a "number of our Staten Islanders returned from the seat of war last week in the 71st, 8th, and 69th New York Regiments."[272] Many were wounded, but thankfully, all of the men originally reported as missing turned up in later dispatches.[273]

Richmond's soldiers were never far from the general engagements of the war. The companies raised by Colonel Tompkins generally were placed in the 132nd, 156th and 175th Regiments. In these units, the men of Castleton, Westfield, Southfield and Northfield fought and died at such faraway places as the Red River, Shenandoah, Cedar Creek and Savannah.[274] Others served in the 72nd Regiment as part of the Excelsior Brigade and took part in the storied Battles of Fredericksburg, Chancellorsville and Gettysburg.[275]

According to nineteenth-century "careful estimates," more than 800 Staten Islanders served in uniform during the Civil War. (With quota of 788 in 1862 alone, though, the number is likely higher.) Of those, the total number estimate of those killed in action or by disease was approximately 180, of which only 40 made it home to be buried in family plots.[276] By comparison, the total number killed is nearly identical to the 171 Staten Islanders who died in the First World War, despite the Island having four times the population and more than five times the number of men in uniform.[277] Only in World War II and on 9/11 would Richmond County lose more of its citizens.

The honor of the highest-ranking Staten Islander to be killed in combat was Brigadier General Stephen Hinsdale Weed, who was mortally wounded on Little Round Top at Gettysburg during one of the most dramatic moments in the Civil War.[278]

Weed was born in Potsdam, New York, and attended West Point but spent the bulk of his childhood living with his uncles in New Dorp Beach.[279] According to an 1874 atlas, the Weeds owned about 180 acres there, their lots straddling Mill Road and Cedar Grove Avenue, and their home stood on present-day Maple Terrace.[280]

Weed commanded units at Bull Run, Antietam, Fredericksburg and Chancellorsville, where he was in charge of fifty-six guns. After the battle, he became one of the youngest generals in the Union army at age twenty-nine.[281]

One the eve of the second day of fighting at Gettysburg, Weed allegedly remarked, "I would rather die on this spot than see those rascals gain one inch of ground." The following day, his men rushed to prop up the Union right flank from the heights of Little Round Top, and as Confederate sharpshooters took positions on Devil's Den across the valley, Weed's brigade "arrived just in time to repulse an assault on that stronghold, the loss of which would have been disastrous in the extreme."[282] The line held, but as Weed stood near the guns of Lieutenant Charles Hazlett's 5th Artillery battery, he was felled by bullet to his chest, leaving him paralyzed. Still alive, he called out for Hazlett, a friend of many years. As the young lieutenant dismounted and leaned over his general, he too was struck in the head, dying instantly, his body slumping on top of Weed's.[283] The spot is marked with a six-foot granite monument stone.

Although General Weed was the highest-ranking Staten Islander killed, he is not the most well known. That honor falls to Robert Gould Shaw, captain of the 54th Massachusetts, whose life was immortalized in the 1989 film *Glory*.

Robert was the son of abolitionists Francis George Shaw and Sarah Blake Sturgis. Originally from Massachusetts, the family moved to Staten Island so Sarah could be under the care of Dr. Samuel Elliot, a renowned optician. She was soon well but found the climate and culture agreeable, and so the Shaws settled on Davis Avenue in Livingston Manor.[284]

The Shaws felt at home among Richmond County's leading antislavery champions, and their children were soon also caught up in the county's politics. Their younger daughter, Josephine Shaw Lowell, went on to become one of New York's leading progressives, dubbed the "grand dame of the social reformers" by the time of her death.[285] Their eldest daughter, Anna, married George William Curtis as he rose in the ranks of publishers and in Republican circles, and the entire Shaw family were part of the founding members of the county's Unitarian Church, which still exists near Snug Harbor.[286]

When war broke, Robert Gould Shaw enlisted with the 7th Regiment, New York State Militia. After the 1863 Emancipation Proclamation, Secretary of War Edwin Stanton called for three regiments of troops composed of

Colonel Robert Gould Shaw, the son of Staten Island abolitionists, led the Massachusetts 54th Regiment, comprising former slaves. *Courtesy of the Library of Congress.*

Black enlisted men, to be commanded by white officers. Shaw's abilities as a soldier and his undeniable abolitionist pedigree made him an obvious choice to lead the first, the famed 54th Massachusetts Infantry.[287]

The men of the 54th consisted of former enslaved, and at least one solider serving under Shaw was a resident of Sandy Ground. Thomas P. Robinson was twenty-one when he joined at the unit's training encampment in Readville, Massachusetts. He listed his occupation as farming and his residence as Staten Island. On July 18, 1863, he was wounded as the regiment stormed Fort Wagner,[288] an imposing structure of earthworks and cannons guarding the entrance to Charleston Harbor. On that day, Colonel Shaw led his men for the final time; he was shot while charging the fort, sword waving and urging his infantrymen forward. Of the 600 soldiers of the 54th, 272 were killed, captured or wounded.[289]

Shaw was buried in a common grave alongside his men, but later that year, once Fort Wagner was in the hands of Union troops, there was an effort to locate his body for its exhumation and separate burial. His father contested, writing to the army that his remains not be disturbed and nor should those he died next to.[290] They granted his wish and only moved all of the bodies when the beach around the fort began to erode.

In 1998, Mayor Rudy Giuliani and the City Council renamed Davis Avenue between Richmond Terrace and Henderson Avenue "Colonel Robert Gould Shaw's Glory Way."[291]

POLITICAL VIOLENCE COMES TO STATEN ISLAND

The engagements of the Civil War may not have made it to State Island's shores, but that did not exempt it from the mob violence that swept up New York City in the summer of 1863, in response to the Conscription Act. Along with Boston, Staten Island was one of the few places draft riots spread after their initial outbreak in Lower Manhattan, although the bulk of historical writing tends to overlook this fact.

The cause of the New York City draft riots is regularly attributed to a growing fear that newly emancipated Blacks would flood northern cities and take the low-skilled jobs then held by the hundreds of thousands of Irish immigrants who began emigrating at an astounding pace in the late 1840s. This particular view did not dissipate even as the city was swept up in the patriotic fervor of 1861, and Democratic newspapers and politicians were eager to stoke the anti-Black flames in their efforts to drum up Irish votes.[292] Even the Catholic hierarchy, immensely influential over the Irish, placed no emphasis on opposing slavery and associated abolitionism with Protestantism.[293] On the stump in November of that year, thirteen months before the Emancipation Proclamation, Mayor Fernando Wood roused a crowd of German and Irish Democrats by reminding them that the Republican Party in power "gives all its sympathy to the black and has none at all to spare for the poor whites of the North….They will get Irishmen and Germans to fill up the regiments and go forth to defend the country… and yet these men have hearts, but not for you, but for the negroes of the South."[294] That December, two Democrats split the vote and allowed Republican George Opdyke to win, but Wood and his angry constituency still secured one-third of the votes.[295]

On Staten Island, the political dynamic was similar. The partisan anger that precluded the election of 1860 did not subside and continued to motivate public sentiment. The county's Irish and German factory workers were equally as concerned as their Manhattan counterparts. Similarly, if these fears underpinned the backdrop of their anger, the spark that directly led disaffected New Yorkers to break out in riots was, as mentioned, the enforcement of the Conscription Act.

The law went into effect in May 1863, and the enrollment went comparatively smooth, despite calls by the *Catholic Metropolitan Record* for armed resistance and Democratic politicians promised a spate of legal challenges. That changed over the summer, just after the victory at Gettysburg. On Saturday July 11, the lottery commenced, and by Sunday morning, poor New Yorkers were reading the lists of those who made up the first 1,236 city draftees.[296] Deepening their rage was the provision that wealthy New Yorkers could purchase an exemption for $300.

On Monday the thirteenth, hours before the start of the second lottery drawing, hundreds of factory workers, laborers, firemen and gang members banded together. By 10:30 a.m., it had become a full-blown insurrection. Mansions were sacked, businesses were burned and the New York Armory was attacked. That night, it turned into a race war, and with shouts of "kill all ni-----!" Black residents were dragged out and stripped, their homes burned. Even the Colored Orphan Asylum was not spared their wrath. By Thursday, 6,000 Federal troops, exhausted from Gettysburg, had restored order in the city by force. Contemporary accounts estimated more than 1,000 deaths, though officially, only 119 bodies were recovered.[297]

News of New York's draft riots hit Staten Island at the same time Richmond County was bracing for its own lottery to choose 400 men. The *Gazette* of July 15 reported that they were "to be taken from our single and married men between the ages of twenty and thirty-five....Very few persons will be exempt—even men of the Gospel are not among the number."[298] However, like their New York neighbors, Richmond's high society types were able to

An engraving depicting a lynching on Clarkson Street during the New York City draft riots in 1863. *Courtesy of the New York Public Library.*

exempt themselves by furnishing substitutes. The following year, for example, 198 Staten Islanders, most all from the oldest and wealthiest families in the county, produced substitutes. Of those who took their places, according to *Morris's Memorial History*, nearly every man bore an Irish surname.[299]

Staten Island was the site of smaller scuffles before the draft riots, but they were limited to the troops on leave and rarely went beyond the camp walls. The largest was a brief mutiny at Camp Sprague earlier that year, after the men spent months in service without receiving enlistment bounties they were due. Many soldiers simply deserted. In one regiment, the 15th Artillery, twenty-two men deserted from Sprague that June,[300] while in another, the 13th Cavalry, thirty-nine enlisted men left too.[301] Other men sought a confrontation, and after a day of rioting on May 13, 1863, one solider lay dead and two others were seriously wounded. Search parties were sent to every outbound ferry to round up escaping perpetrators and drag them back to camp. Twenty-eight of the ringleaders were caught trying to enter New Jersey and were imprisoned on Governor's Island.[302] Two months later, with the soldiers still in poor spirits, the citizens of Staten Island were concerned about their safety as the resentment stewed over the draft. The situation was ready to explode, and when the news of the Manhattan riots finally reached the Island, it did.

Black Islanders were the first to be targeted as "sober counsels wavered and the influence of men of means was weak."[303] On Tuesday, July 14, a mob formed on McKeon Street in Stapleton. What is now the site of the Stapleton Playground was then a row of homes that housed a large concentration of African Americans, along with their church. After numerous verbal threats of burning and lynching, most of the residents fled into the woods and did not return for days.[304]

Just down the street, the mob was less subdued. Nearly two hundred young men broke into the recruiting hall of the Tompkins Lyceum on Van Duzer Street and the army drill room at Stapleton Landing and robbed a stock of muskets. Now armed, the pack made its way to the railway depot at Vanderbilt's Landing and burned it to the ground. Two fire companies that responded were held back at gunpoint.[305]

A separate mob formed at Factoryville, marched eastward to shouts of "No Draft!" and broke into two businesses linked to abolitionists. The first was owned by a Black man named Green, formerly a butler to the Shaw family but who had since opened a thriving ice cream and cake business. The mob made its way inside his store and "did not leave two sticks of it together."[306] The other was a drugstore belonging to a neighboring abolitionist, William

Christie. They set fire to the place, believing that Green might have been hiding inside, but luckily he was already gone. They continued eastward and stopped at the doors of St. Peter's Church but were persuaded to retire for the night by Father James Conran.[307]

The following night, as headlines around the region declared a "Riot on Staten Island,"[308] the mob resumed its diabolical work. It returned to McKeon Street and broke the windows of nearly every vacant house, spewing contents into the street. The house of David Wormsley, who had once advocated for the arming of Black residents, was burned to the ground. A small grocery store was looted and a neighboring church set ablaze, albeit unsuccessfully. An elderly Black man was beaten in the street, while another, a coachman working nearby, was attacked and only narrowly escaped alive.[309]

On Thursday the sixteenth, under orders from Governor Horatio Seymour, regular troops were ordered to Staten Island from Lower Manhattan, and the 6th New York Volunteers were called into service from Camp Sprague. Colonel William Wilson was ordered to take command of all forces in Richmond County, with the purpose of "suppressing riots and maintaining law and order."[310]

The troops were visible throughout the Island, and for a few days mass gatherings were limited. A detachment had to be posted at the Richmondtown Courthouse to protect a jailed Black prisoner after a local mob arrived with the intention of issuing a punishment without a trial by jury. He was soon transferred to the Tombs prison in Manhattan.

Despite their visibility, the troops could not prevent all depredations. Martin Gay, the son of Sydney Howard Gay and an eyewitness to the riots, reported that at least one "old woman who sold peanuts and apples" at the ferry landing had been killed. He had heard from others that she was kicked around "like a football."[311] Nearby in Castleton, a man named John Ryan was beaten and robbed of his clothes while walking home from work. The pack finally attempted to loot a local saloon before the authorities could arrive.[312]

By July 18, Governor Seymour believed that things had subsided enough to relieve some of the troops, and he ordered the men of the 6th Volunteers back to their homes.[313] Just two days later, he was proven wrong.

One of the units dispatched to quell the riots in New York City during the previous week was the 11th Volunteer Infantry, also known as the "Fire Zouaves." Their enlistments had expired, and by July 18, they were back at their camp in New Dorp reorganizing into a new regiment with other veterans. The 11th was made up predominantly of New York firemen, and thus its men were singled out as traitors by their local fire company comrades who formed the backbone of the ranks of the riotous mob. Making matters worse, the Zouaves may have been on edge and eager to pick a fight with those they saw as agitators, as the New York City mob was responsible for the death of their beloved colonel, Henry O'Brien, just days earlier.[314]

On Monday evening, July 20, after a busy couple of days, a company of about one hundred men of the 11th disembarked the ferry from Manhattan at Vanderbilt's Landing to await the train to return them to camp. As soldiers occasionally do, three men wandered down the railroad tracks and into a nearby drinking establishment on the western end of Wood Road (now St. Mary's Avenue), hoping to meet a few acquaintances.[315]

Accounts vary as to what happened next. New York City newspapers like the *Evening Post* and its Republican editor, William Cullen Bryant, backed the Zouaves' statement that they were "set upon" by "about twenty ruffians."[316] The *New York Herald* also blamed the mob, and the *Daily Tribune* said they were chased by "some rough fellows residing in the vicinity, who inquired 'What in the h--l they were doing there?'" and were pelted with stones.[317]

Both the *Richmond County Gazette* and the contemporary chronicler, Richard Bayles, blamed the troops. Yet regardless of who started it, the soldiers fired at least one shot in the direction of a young boy, and the mob soon set upon them in revenge.[318]

At least one of the three Zouaves got away to alert the rest of his company. By the time they returned, the other two soldiers, Privates John Cook and John Welsh, had been beaten and stabbed. Welsh got the worst of it. "His abdomen was ripped open, so that his intestines and stomach protruded, and his skull was beaten in,"[319] likely with his own musket. He was taken to the nearby Seaman's Retreat (the site of Bayley Seton Hospital),[320] where he lingered until "death put an end to his sufferings."[321]

Cook was hospitalized as well. He received six stab wounds, and his case was considered hopeless.[322] The regimental records indicate that he was eventually taken to the Ladies' Home General Hospital in New York City, where he died on September 14.[323]

During the scuffle, Cook fired a shot and believed he hit one of the ruffians. By that time, the company had traveled just a short distance by train when it stopped at some point between Wood Road and the landing. According to the sworn testimony of an eyewitness, "an officer entered the cars and ordered the soldiers out.…Immediately we heard the report of firearms, and we all endeavored to escape from danger."[324]

The "Washington Greys," 8th Regiment of New York State, at camp on Staten Island just prior to the start of the war. *Courtesy of the Library of Congress.*

Another eyewitness claimed that at least fifty shots were fired, with some of the balls hitting his home. The soldiers began searching for the perpetrators, raiding doors along Wood Avenue and dragging people and property outside. More than twenty people were taken prisoner. In the scuffle, he saw Charles Murphy running down the street and was quickly followed by several soldiers. One of them took deliberate aim and shot; soon word came that he had been killed.[325] The riot was over.

Murphy's death caused further outrage on Staten Island. A grand jury was formed, and the high character of both Cook and Walsh were attested to. However, the jury found that Murphy had nothing to do with the original fracas, and although it could not determine which soldier committed the crime, it blamed the intoxication of the group and the failure of the officers to corral their men.[326]

Whether it is related to the riot of July 20 or not is unknown, but during the first week of August, a suspicious fire broke out at Camp Sprague. Most suspected arson, but it was unclear whether it had been the work of a dissatisfied soldier, a local thug or even a Southern sympathizer.[327] The library, quartermaster's store and more than half the barracks were destroyed.[328]

The total damage from all of the riots was significant, and the courts placed the bulk of the burden on Richmond County for failing to protect its inhabitants. The repairs and the cost to adjudicate the claims totaled more than $27,000, with the railroad receiving $1,366 and the Wormsley family, the only Black family to be compensated, receiving more than $5,000 for their home and its contents.[329]

That Richmond County had to pay these damages certainly did not help its financial situation. The war had hurt the Island's coffers; the cost of issuing bonds to pay the bounties and care for enlisted families totaled $895,000.[330] At its end, Staten Island was left heavy in debt, wrought with political turmoil and its industries dying for want of men and materiel. All that would soon change.

CHAPTER 3

Island Oasis

A t war's end, Richmond County found itself short of cash and people. Despite its inviting hills, comparably cheap real estate prices and convenient access to the waterways, Staten Island did not see the same population boom that took shape in neighboring counties around New York Harbor. Between 1860 and 1870, its population grew by just 7,000, whereas Westchester added 32,000 and Hudson County, New Jersey, doubled to 68,000 people. Brooklyn grew by a whopping 140,000.[331]

The stagnant economic environment did little to undo the political unease that existed in antebellum Staten Island. As the war wrapped up, dissatisfaction over the handling of war debt and the poor outlook for repaying it led to a seismic shift in local politics. Three out of the five town supervisors were thrown out of office in 1865.[332]

The significance of this cannot be understated, as the county government was operated, at this time, by a board of town supervisors, governing Richmond alongside a few countywide officers. The new supervisors were largely influenced by "Honest" John Thompson, who along with Daniel Low and other reformers formed the Island's Taxpayers Association the prior year with the intention of stabilizing the county's finances and weeding out any rotten apples within government. The coalition brought charges of mismanagement against the county treasurer, and in 1867, Peter S. Wandel, Esq., was forced to resign in shame.[333] It was clearly a new political era.

Staten Islanders of the 1870s sought to improve the county as the population began to increase, both from outside sources in New York City and Albany and from the resources that those within the county could muster themselves. Unfortunately, off-Island interest in Richmond's infrastructure would wane during this period, despite the formation of a commission to come up with grand plans. What projects did materialize were nearly always the result of Staten Island's own citizens, pushing its progress. In the process, Staten Island became a destination for regional tourism, athletics and entertainment.

The Commission

Tourism would not solve the larger problem of how to populate Staten Island, grow its economy or improve its infrastructure. John Decker, a Republican Assembly member and scion of one of the Island's oldest families,[334] appealed to the legislature for help in developing "a plan for improvements on Staten Island, in respect to roads, avenues and parks, and means of transportation and communication to and from said island."[335] Like many others, Decker realized that the county needed some type infrastructure plan, which would likely require state funding.

The bill that passed the legislature in 1870 authorized $5,000 to be spent on a commission with two purposes. The first was to uncover what caused Staten Island to lag behind its neighbors in terms of development, and the second was to make recommendations for its improvement. The members included both Islanders and outsiders. Many prominent business and civic leaders were among the ninety-five named in the bill, including familiar individuals like Shaw, Curtis, Brooks and J.J. Clute, who was writing his *Annals of Staten Island*,[336] as well as Balthazar Kreischer, William Vanderbilt and John S. Westervelt, who had grown prosperous since serving as the chief health officer of the quarantine.[337]

Equally prominent among Richmond County's new planning commission were reformers plucked from New York's high society and were associated with that city's own efforts at centralized planning. Robert Roosevelt, a member of Congress and staunch anti-Tammany Democrat,[338] also had a seat on the commission, as did James Gordon Bennett Jr., a wealthy, yacht racing, Arctic-exploring, playboy-publisher of the *New York Herald*.[339] But the most prominent spots on the commission were reserved for Andrew Haswell Green and Frederick Law Olmsted.[340] Olmsted, as mentioned earlier, was a famous landscape architect who resided for many years on his family's farm on the south shore. Green was one of the city's most well-known civic reformers, earning the frequent ire of the Tammany bunch. As the *Times* would remember, "His name had been associated with some of the most creditable enterprises ever devised for the benefit of the city."[341] In 1870, the year the Improvement Commission formed, both were putting the finishing touches on Central Park: Olmsted giving the landscape its beauty and Green, the hard-nosed controller and general manager, pushing the project to completion despite challenges from money, materials, engineering and corrupt politicians.[342]

Frederick Law Olmsted, designer of Central Park, was appointed to the 1871 Richmond County Planning Commission. *Courtesy of the New York Public Library.*

In January 1871, just eight months after it was charged, the committee returned a report to the legislature. Its work, the *Report of a Preliminary Scheme of Improvements*, was the first attempt to form a centralized plan of Staten Island's future expansion and was arguably the first time New York's authorities took any interest in improving the county for development since the colonial period.[343]

Foremost among its charges, the Island suffered from unhealthy conditions, which they attributed to its "malarial troubles" from poor drainage. In fact, they concluded, "If Staten Island can be freed from malaria, it will be a comparatively easy matter to make it the healthiest, and at the same time the most convenient and most beautiful suburb of New York."[344]

To solve this, they recommended a system of fifteen-inch-diameter pipes at half-mile intervals, roughly coinciding with existing and proposed roadbeds, to be dug into the earth in order to drain the island's stagnant ponds and mucky swamps. Natural watercourses would also be improved on and dug out, to serve both scenic and functional purposes.[345] To complement some of these watercourses, the commission envisioned a system of public parks, which eventually became Clove Lakes and Silver Lake Park. Sadly, as Islanders can now attest, much of this infrastructure work was not begun for nearly one hundred years, and sewer pipes and bluebelts are still being constructed well into the twenty-first century.

The second problem they hoped to address was "the radical defects of the present system of communication with New York."[346] The ferry service in the 1870s was an inadequate and unreliable operation, one that simply could not guarantee regular service with Manhattan. The commission adopted a proposal put forward by "Honest" John Thompson: rather than have ferries operate from existing wharfs at Vanderbilt's Landing, Port Richmond and sites even farther away, a new singular operation should open from the nearest point to its destination at New Brighton Point (the name St. George was not yet used). This would provide the most reliable service with the shortest distance and would be least hampered by ice, inclement weather and shipping.[347] The chief reason New Brighton Point did not have an existing ferry service was the inaccessibility of its waterfront. The town, even in the present day, is set on a hill, and any landing site would require horse-drawn wagons to rise and descend at too steep of an incline. To address this, they proposed grading new and existing roads from the heights of the Island to New Brighton and Tompkinsville.[348]

At New Brighton Point, to accommodate all of the carriages awaiting future ferries, the commission proposed a grand waterfront plaza, double the size of a football field, from which the Island's three new highways would spring out. Each would be "not less than one hundred feet wide," with the largest running from New Brighton along the Island's spine toward Tottenville; the second along the north shore toward Elizabethtown; and the third to run below the escarpment, tracing the path of modern Richmond and Amboy Roads, with a branch running off toward Richmondtown. To complete the system of highways, they proposed a Shore Road, also of one hundred feet in width, to run along the New Dorp plains south toward Tottenville and then up the west shore.[349]

If the Island could be effectively drained and roads constructed, the commissioners hoped that twenty thousand "detached villas and cottages" would be built for "twenty thousand families glad to buy them at once, at prices a good deal more than double the present average value of all the land on Staten Island."[350] These would be divided by lots sized between five acres for the pricier villas and one acre for the smaller properties in less desirable areas.[351] The commission's true purpose of encouraging real estate speculation by wealthy New Yorkers was poorly veiled.

Improving Transit

Despite the commissioners favoring the development of highways, the construction they expected was not undertaken. An extensive network of public roadways would wait until the era of cars and Robert Moses. The ferry system, however, was improved. The commission condemned the current condition of the boats and stressed the need to take precautions against accidents. Unfortunately, this concern proved deadly prophetic just months after the report was published, and it is fair to say that the eventual improvement of the Island's ferry service was born out of one of the most tragic incidents in the county's history rather than any blue ribbon plan.

On a stifling July 30, 1871, four hundred people boarded the Staten Island ferry steamer *Westfield* and awaited their departure toward what they hoped would be a pleasant Sunday afternoon on the Staten Island shore. At 1:30 p.m., its captain was preparing to depart a slip at Whitehall when its boiler exploded, destroying nearly the entire fore-end of the ship and sending its pilothouse and cabins hurtling fifty feet away. Hundreds were immediately killed or blasted out into the water, where they clung to broken planks and tried their best to stay afloat.[352] Many drowned as eyewitnesses from shore and on an adjacent steamer, the *Hamilton*, watched in terror and were unable to help. Five minutes passed before a flotilla of rowboats and the police boat *Seneca* arrived to what one witness described in the *Evening Post*:

> *After the explosion, those of her passengers who had not been hurled into the air were exposed to the horrors of steam, as the dock and ferryhouse were obscured by a thick cloud of the escaping vapor. The screams of the women and children, wild with pain and terror, were indescribable. They made the blood of the hearers run cold, and many persons in the street put their fingers to their ears, unable to bear the agonizing sounds.*[353]

The dead included dozens of women and children. Entire families were wiped out. More than one hundred injured victims, including unidentified children, were brought to Bellevue and Centre Street Hospitals, where many died in agony. In all, 104 perished, the majority coming from the working-class neighborhoods of Lower Manhattan and Brooklyn.[354]

Within days, the investigation began, and the vessel's owner, Jacob Vanderbilt, was on the witness stand. Jacob had bought the operation of the ferries from the landing and the new Staten Island Railroad from his brother, Cornelius, just years before. Vanderbilt believed that the boiler on the *Westfield* was better than that of his other boats, as it was made from a higher-quality iron that was only available before the war.[355] His attempts at skirting blame did not register well with the public, nor did it sway a grand jury. A warrant was issued, and he was arrested along with the other officers of the company.[356] While he served no jail time, Jacob Vanderbilt's conglomerate over the Staten Island Railroad and east shore ferry operations

On July 30, 1871, the ferryboat *Westfield* exploded while pulling into its slip, killing 104 people. *Courtesy of the New York Public Library.*

went bust and faced foreclosure in 1872. It was purchased for pennies on the dollar by his chief rival, George Law.[357]

East shore ferries had been connecting Staten Island with New York for more than two hundred years but reached a peak during the mid-nineteenth century, when Law held a considerable monopoly over service to Lower Manhattan. Starting with nine steamboats from a rented slip in Whitehall in 1853, the Staten Island Ferry Company ran regular services to Tompkinsville, Stapleton and Vanderbilt's Landing, which he respectively renamed the First, Second and Third Landings to New York. The original fare was six cents, although Law raised it to ten in 1863.[358]

Staten Islanders soon grew frustrated with Law's chokehold on East Shore service, especially as quality dissipated with his competition. The *Gazette* was sharply critical of "the uncleanly condition of the boats" in 1863, claiming that "railroad passengers find themselves just one minute too late" and managers "care nothing for the accommodation of the public." The people of Staten Island, they declared, are "virtually at the mercy of George Law. He directs our incomings and outgoings; he tells us what we may do, and what we cannot possibly be permitted to attempt; he imposes grievous burdens upon the island and its people."[359]

For relief, Staten Islanders looked to an unlikely champion, Manhattan assemblyman Julius Korn. It was the Sixth District Democrat and not Staten Island's own representative, Theodore Frean, who presented "two petitions of inhabitants of Richmond County, for the passage of a law to regulate the ferries between New York and Staten Island."[360] Frean

George Law was a financier who owned numerous steamboat lines, eventually including the right to operate between Staten Island and Manhattan. *Courtesy of the Library of Congress.*

submitted his own bill that year,[361] but Korn's legislation had the effect of radically altering the monopoly on service. In February 1864, the Staten Island Ferry Company fell into the possession of the Staten Island Railroad Company and the Vanderbilts.[362]

East shore service, in coordination with the railroad, would exist under a separate corporate umbrella and was eventually consolidated with all service from the north shore. Until that point, separate steamboat licensees for Whitehall to north shore routes had existed since the 1820s, alongside the *Bellona*, which ran between Elizabethtown and Mersereau's Ferry in Port Richmond.[363] By 1833, advertisements for new homes in the *Richmond County Free Press* were boasting a "three minute walk of Mersereau's Ferry."[364] Six departures per day was enough to entice many prospective buyers. Later that decade, the *Water Witch*, *Cinderella* and *Staten Islander* were all making daily runs to Port Richmond, Snug Harbor and New Brighton.[365]

In 1860, a competing North Shore Ferry Company opened, operating as "The People's Line," and offered a cheaper and more convenient option for north shore travelers. Instead of landing solely at Whitehall, these also stopped along the Hudson waterfront. But after decades of price battles, collisions, gouging and undercutting, all of the north shore lines were consolidated in 1884 under the umbrella of the New York and Staten Island Steamboat Company,[366] under the impetus of two Staten Islanders, William Pendleton and Erastus Wiman[367]—the latter arguably being the most prominent businessman in the county.

By the early 1880s, the problems of the privately owned ferryboats had reached a fever pitch, and the number of Islanders commuting to Manhattan increased dramatically. The problem called for a mass consolidation of lines going to the city, more reliable service and, most importantly, coordination with the Staten Island Railroad.

The idea of including all of the lines serving Staten Island was never considered, and those operating to New Jersey continued unchanged. The Bergen Point and Port Richmond ferry connected residents with the Central Railroad of New Jersey, which gave them an alternate route to New York, and it was a popular method, while the north shore–New York boats faced their reliability problems in the 1870s. Along the West Shore, regular steamboats connected Elizabeth and Mariners Harbor, Rossville and New Brunswick and all elsewhere in between. There had been rowboat ferries between Tottenville and Amboy since 1708, and the first steamboat began operating in 1860.[368] Tottenville became a major stop on routes between New York, Perth Amboy and New Brunswick and was served by six boats at its peak.[369]

Still, the priority for Staten Islanders was to streamline the service available to New York City. The visionary and driving force behind the consolidation of all North and East shore ferries with the Staten Island Railroad was Erastus Wiman, a Canadian-born businessman who, in partnership with the Baltimore & Ohio Railroad, formed the Staten Island Rapid Transit Railway Company in 1883. The plan was relatively simple: combine the existing Staten Island Railroad with new branches on the north shore and to South

A newspaper clipping announced the grave illness of Erastus Wiman, arguably the most influential Staten Islander of the nineteenth century. *Courtesy of the New York Public Library.*

Beach and have them all join together at one large terminal for all Staten Island–New York ferryboats.[370]

The site chosen for the new slips and rail yards was at the extreme northeastern tip of Staten Island, to the east of New Brighton and above Tompkinsville, but the property was still owned by George Law. As legend has it, Wiman promised that he would "canonize him" if Law granted the Rapid Transit company permission to lease the land. The result was the town of "St. George."[371]

By the time Richard Bayles was writing his *History of Richmond County*, construction was well underway. "[A]n area of several acres of ground has been made out from the shore to afford room for terminal facilities. Piers have been erected, extending some six hundred feet into the water, and terminating in two large ferry slips."[372] In order to avoid encroaching on the property surrounding a lighthouse service depot owned by the federal government, Wiman also had to construct a tunnel between Tompkinsville and the new terminal of nearly six hundred feet in length, wide enough for two tracks and protected by massive walls of masonry on each side.[373]

On July 31, 1884, the Staten Island Rapid Transit Railway Company began its ninety-nine year lease of the former Staten Island Railway line with the opening of the first new stretch between Vanderbilt's Landing and the St. George Terminal. Ira K. Morris, author of *Morris's Memorial History of Staten Island*, was one of the passengers who took the train's inaugural run without much fanfare, "as it came on its regular time from Tottenville."[374]

Both the South Beach and the north shore branches opened in 1886, but the idea of operating a rail line along the north shore waterfront was not new. As early as 1860, almost as soon as the main line of the Staten Island Railway opened, north shore residents were publicly demanding a new line be extended nine miles, in an "already thickly populated" route, from the Narrows to Mariners Harbor. Instead of using steam engines, they proposed a horse-drawn railroad, which could be more cheaply and easily built.[375] The Staten Island Horse Railroad Company formed in 1863 and made a formal proposal to county leaders, and while the idea proved popular to those more generally along the route, it faced steep opposition from homeowners with homes fronting directly on the line.[376]

The *Gazette* announced the opening of the line on November 27, 1867,[377] but its success was short-lived. The "Shore Line" line was unable to be completed in several spots due to a shortage of railroad ties, and gaps and section closures were the norm for the first year. Angry Islanders wrote letters to local papers demanding the tracks be removed if they were to continue to be as infrequently used and left in disrepair. Within a year, the company was in foreclosure and sold to a new corporation, the Staten Island Shore Railroad Company, which ran it more successfully for two decades.[378]

That twenty-year stretch also saw the development of several other horse-car railroads throughout the Island. One route ran from the West Brighton docks to Castleton Corners, then called "Four Corners," and stopped roughly where the Todt Hill Houses now sit.[379] There had been a proposal to extend a similar route farther south, along Rockland Avenue before following a horseshoe bend around to Richmondtown and Greenridge. It was never built.[380] Another horse-car line extended from Stapleton to Concord, following Broad Street and Richmond Road, and a third serviced the shoreline between South Beach and a number of beach hotels and camps farther south,[381] each station having a quaint name like "Crabtree Station," "Camp Warren," "Ocean Breeze," "Bungalow Town" and "Poppy Joe Island."[382]

Still, Wiman understood that horse-car lines were inefficient, and a steam train connection to his new ferry terminal was still needed. When the Rapid Transit Company began serving the north shore in February 1886, with stops in New Brighton, Snug Harbor, West New Brighton, Port Richmond and Elm Park, it became an instant success.[383] As one contemporary noted, "The people along the North Shore in particular celebrated that event"[384]—their commute to New York City had become reliably shorter.

Erastus Wiman's vision extended to the west as well. Although a bridge linking Staten Island with New Jersey had not been attempted since the British used a pontoon bridge during the Revolution, Wiman saw the value in connecting passengers with the Jersey Central Railroad and connecting industry with the coal, iron and oil freight operations of New Jersey and Pennsylvania. He found a willing partner in the B&O Railroad. The route would cross the Arthur Kill at Howland Hook and run about five miles through Linden and Roselle Park before merging at Cranford Junction.[385] This link would give Manhattan and Brooklyn rail passengers a new option for westward. More significantly, Wiman believed that by tying into the infrastructure of New Jersey, Richmond County could become a strong competitor to other New York counties around the harbor and help attract new factories and freight operations to its shores.

The bridge was completed on June 13, 1888, but the first passenger train to cross the Arthur Kill came on New Year's Day 1890. At the time of its construction, it was the largest swingbridge in the world, and hundreds came to witness and celebrate its test run. The *Times* reported, "It required just four and a half minutes to turn the bridge for the first time, but on the second trial the feat was accomplished in three minutes." Perhaps more astonishing, "it required just four weeks to erect the draw span, and two weeks longer to put the machinery in order," during which "not a single accident occurred."[386] The *Gazette* praised the "noble structure consisting of five pillars of solid masonry" and remarked that it "worked like a charm…there was not a difference of a quarter of an inch in the calculations."[387] Interestingly, the opposition to what would be the first link between New York and its neighbor came from the state of New Jersey. Its industrialists feared competition from the extended B&O line and used every possible legal means to prevent it, including the charge that it would impede navigation.[388] In response, the *Gazette* mockingly ran the headline, "State Wedded Unto State: Imperial New York Leads New Jersey, an Unwilling Bride, to the Altar."[389]

Staten Island Summer

To fill his railroad cars and ferries, Wiman sought to bring not only locals to New York and New Jersey but also regular visitors to Staten Island's beaches and rolling hills. For St. George, he published an advertising pamphlet entitled "Picturesque Staten Island," whose cover depicted his ferry terminal and steam locomotive, as well as a picture of the newly constructed grandstand,[390] where visitors could see "Cappa's Seventh Regiment Band of sixty pieces."[391] Wiman had also bought the Metropolitan Baseball Club in 1886 for $25,000. He billed the Mets (the namesake of the current team) as a "Famous Baseball Team," who for one season played their games at the St. George Cricket Grounds the following year.[392]

The Metropolitan Baseball Club, the precursor to the Mets, playing at their grounds in St. George in the 1880s. *Courtesy of the New York Public Library.*

Wiman also electrified St. George to power his amusements, including "wonderful fountains…all illuminated from the mysterious subterranean chamber by powerful electric lights, shining through lenses of all colors, changed with kaleidoscopic rapidity."[393] Additionally, he spent $35,000 on an "immense casino," three stories high, larger than a football field, built of iron and with seating for five thousand overlooking the harbor.[394]

Wiman wanted folks from around the region to use his rails and ferries to see a regular array of traveling shows, and he spared no expense in getting the best acts. In conjunction with the Kiralfy Brothers, then well-known producers, his audiences were dazzled by *The Fall of Babylon* in 1887 and *The Fall of Rome* in 1888. The latter had more than two thousand performers and featured a herd of elephants stabled on Jersey Street.[395]

Yet the Kiralfy Brothers cannot claim to have brought the most famous show of its day to Richmond County. That honor goes to one who still reigns high in American popular memory. In Wiman's own memoirs, he recalled the day in 1885 when he found a "plain-looking countryman…a cross between a brakeman and a farmer," waiting to see him on a bench outside of his office. Claiming to have come all the way from Omaha, he said, "I am John Burke, general manager for the Hon. Wm. F. Cody, usually known as 'Buffalo Bill,' and I have been sent on to discover what are the chances for an alliance with the new Rapid Transit movement on Staten Island."[396]

Realizing that the St. George facilities would be insufficient, he whisked Burke west along the north shore line, still under construction, to a beautiful piece of land adjacent to a planned railway stop. Burke believed that the small grove of property in present-day Mariners Harbor could serve as the perfect spot for next summer's show. Burke agreed and Wiman purchased the property.[397]

According to Wiman's memory, it was Cody himself who named the station and surrounding land "Erastina," but given the resemblance to the property owner's first name, that claim may be an exaggeration. Regardless, *Buffalo Bill's Wild West* opened in June and spent four successful months of 1886 there.[398] In Wiman's estimation, it brought 1.5 million riders[399] on board "The Buffalo Bill Express," a clever name he used to market the north shore trains servicing the audiences.[400] It was, he claimed, "a larger number of persons than had ever before been known to visit Staten Island."[401] On site, he constructed seating for 20,000 and a four-thousand-square-foot restaurant pavilion to accommodate throngs of visitors. The show consisted of more than two hundred horses, a herd of cattle, 100 Native American performers and 40 "cow-boys and other men of the plain."[402] The *Herald*

Buck Taylor, one of the stars of Buffalo Bill's Wild West Show, poses with fellow actors and their teepees at Erastina in 1888. *Courtesy of the McCracken Research Library.*

described the visitors from New York as coming in "train after train packed full of sweltering humanity," yet enjoying the "rolling hills clothed in fresh greenness and walled with dark woods."[403] The *Richmond County Advance* was more perceptive of the show, noting that it "opened up that hitherto almost unknown section of our beautiful Island to the great public, the result of which is already, and will be in the future, an increased demand for real estate and building lots."[404]

That notion proved true. Real estate advertisements popped up in New York newspapers with increasing frequency, offering "country seats"[405] near Clifton or a "first-class house"[406] in New Brighton; others boasted of the Island's amenities like "bathing, boating and fishing."[407] Richmond County would add nearly fifteen thousand new residents by 1890.[408]

Wiman certainly opened up Staten Island to New Yorkers in ways that had never before been seen. But in reality, ever since wealthy families were buying estates and summer homes on the hills in the decades before the Civil War, city dwellers of lesser means had already been taking steamboats across the bay for rest and relaxation. Even an 1834 article on New York's most notable recreation spots in the *Dublin Penny Journal* noted that visitors are

On the Sand, Midland Beach.   Staten Island, N. Y.

Midland Beach saw its peak as a summer destination toward to the end of the century, once it was more accessible through ferries, trains and trolleys. *Courtesy of the New York Public Library.*

greeted with "the most sublime prospect that can be imagined" and rated the county's heights as on par with the scenic Hudson Highlands.[409]

South Beach soon became a booming resort town, boasting beer gardens, shooting galleries, bathing areas, Ferris wheels, theaters and dance halls. In 1881, a hot weekend could see up to 100,000 visitors in twenty-five separate hotels and a bevy of bathing pavilions.[410]

Midland Beach saw its growth occur slightly later. The 1874 atlas shows few homes along Lincoln Avenue, then called Red Lane.[411] Yet just to the south, the salt air and summer winds were drawing families to a small collection of bungalows among sandy beaches and tidal pools. The members of the Westchester Walking Club described the scene for the *New York Herald* in 1879: "Children were swinging in trees…and on a green level boy of large growth were waxing warm in the unsabbatarian pursuit of a game of baseball. The place was Cedar Grove, which during the summer months is a favorite resort."[412] Nearby, Staten Islanders and day-trippers crowded into the grandstands of a three-quarter mile horse racing track built in the 1850s on land belonging to William Vanderbilt[413] that eventually became Miller Field. Just up New Dorp Lane, the Seaview Park Association owned and operated a smaller half-mile racing track.[414]

As the nineteenth century waned, the Staten Island shore boomed. Tourism steadily increased decade after decade until its peak in the early twentieth century. In the 1890s, Midland Beach finally caught up to South Beach as the east shore branch of the Staten Island railroad reached its Ocean Breeze depot, just feet from the first Midland Beach attractions. Tourists could also access the new resort area through one of the latest transportation improvements to grace the Island: the electric trolley.

The first trolley line on the Island ran in 1892 along Jewett Avenue between Port Richmond and a new development around Prohibition

Park. That neighborhood, eventually known as Westerleigh, was originally populated by followers of the temperance movement, and many of its streets still bear the names of prominent prohibitionists like Neal Dow and Mary Livermore.[415] Within a few short years, trolley lines were crossing nearly every quarter of the Island and serving primarily the seaside attractions.[416] When the Midland Beach line opened in March 1896, the *New York Tribune* claimed that "a large number of people" visited on its first day.[417]

Still, the existing transportation proved insufficient to meet the demand, and area newspapers ran stories highlighting the stress on Staten Island's transit network.[418] The *Richmond County Advance* ran the headline "Trolley Cars Crowded,"[419] and on July 4, 1897, when a record thirty-thousand-person crowd turned up in Midland Beach and "every bathing suit was rented," the *Tribune* reported, "The trolley companies ran a number of extra cars and only one accident occurred. An Italian stepped off a running car on Richmond Road and had his head cut."[420] In response, a new pier was completed by 1900 at the foot of Lincoln Avenue for direct service from Manhattan.[421] However, the solution only brought even more crowds.

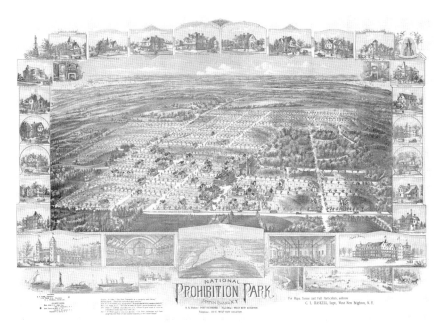

An advertisement for vacant lots in Prohibition Park, demonstrating stately homes and public buildings to be found there. The neighborhood founded on temperance eventually became Westerleigh, a modern neighborhood with several popular bars. *Courtesy of the New York Public Library.*

Richmond County's beach resorts were popular with New York families of all castes, but the fanfare was also a favorite of soldiers while on leave from Fort Wadsworth and other harbor batteries. This was especially true during the Spanish-American War, when forts all housed full garrisons. As the *Advance* reported, their presence was met with different sentiments from Staten Islanders of each gender. "Large crowds of soldiers congregate at South Beach in the dance halls and other places of amusement. Their showy uniforms attract the attention of the women who frequent those places, and as a consequence a keen rivalry exists between citizens and soldiers."[422] In the summer of 1900, the police were forced to tamper a "riot" that broke out between soldiers of the 5th Artillery and a group of smooth-talking Port Richmond dockworkers who had seemingly won the affections of a group of young ladies.[423]

Courting the opposite sex was not the only past-time visitors enjoyed at the turn of the century. As amateur fishing became popular, anglers from the region flocked to "relatively famous" hotels in Great Kills harbor and Prince's Bay, "which catered to their wants in boats, bait, and food."[424] Four hotels popped up in Great Kills to cater to fisherman in the late nineteenth century, with two more In Prince's Bay. The end of Joline Avenue in Tottenville was home to the New York Fishing Club.[425] Staten Island youths earned extra money selling bloodworms to eager sportsmen, and others made sure they were in good spirits.[426] Alcohol was never in short supply, and in one case at the turn of the century, three drunken amateur fishermen were arrested for assaulting their charter captain after a slow day on the water.[427] For the more discerning family, they could enjoy days of recreation on the sixty-acre Woods of Arden resort on the south shore, where "the management invites the best class of pleasure-seekers only."[428] From its office in Lower Manhattan, the resort boasted in newspaper ads of the "quietist and coolest place for an afternoon picnic,"[429] as well as swings, boats, bathing, croquet, baseball and refreshments; additionally, of course, gentlemen could be assured "a fine sport may be had with the rod and the line."[430] The road that led from the Amboy Road to the seaside property still retains the name.

Another sport that drew regular crowds to Richmond County was cricket, which had a presence well before the outbreak of the Civil War. While the Staten Island Cricket Club claims its origin to be in 1872, making it the oldest club in the United States still in existence,[431] the sport, and even the club's name, was recorded here much earlier. To avoid confusion with the white-collar New Brighton Cricket Club, the New Brighton Mechanics Club, which was "principally composed of players whose livelihood is acquired by personal labor," had originally changed its name to the Staten Island Cricket Club in 1858.[432] The club was soon regularly playing matches against other cities, and by 1877, its escapades against teams from all over the East Coast were regularly featured in the *New York Times*.[433] The paper recorded the first match played at the new grounds in present-day Walker Park, where matches are still held, as an intramural match between the American-born and English members of the club. Afterward, they christened their new clubhouse with hearty drinking.[434]

Ironically, the Cricket Club was responsible, perhaps more so than any other organization, for introducing the modern game of tennis to the United States from Britain.

Mary Ewing Outerbridge was the seventh child born into the wealthy Bermuda family of Alexander Ewing Outerbridge. By the 1870s, they had moved to Westervelt Avenue in the town of Castleton,[435] where she and her siblings became members of the club. While visiting Bermuda in 1874, she fell in love with a game played among British army officers involving volleying a ball over a net.[436] Her determination to bring it home was briefly stalled when customs agents came upon a long narrow net and oddly shaped woven tools. While she tried to explain that it was for a sport called *sphairistiké*, Greek for "playing at ball," they refused to allow it ashore. But her brother, A. Emilius Outerbridge, was a local shipping executive and called in favors to his friends down at the docks. Soon dozens of well-appointed Staten Islanders could be seen bouncing a ball over a net on top of an hourglass-shaped court of green spring grass. While the name *sphairistiké* didn't stick, tennis was here to stay.[437]

Before long, tennis clubs were formed in nearby cities from Newport to New Orleans, as the game's smooth, graceful motions and small talk–permitting pace made it popular among the American bourgeoisie. Although at least five other separate individuals or clubs claim to have been the first to bring tennis to the United States in the 1870s, when it came time for the sport's first national tournament, it was Outerbridge and the Staten Island Cricket Club that played host.[438]

In its early years, and despite the influence of Mary Ewing Outerbridge, tennis was a sport dominated by upper-class men. It was not until 1887 that the first women's tournament was held, but sadly, Mary would not live to see it. She died the previous year at the age of thirty-four.[439] For many years, her contribution to the sport had gone largely unnoticed, both on Staten Island and out in the broader tennis community. Her name has even been overshadowed by her younger brother, Eugenius Outerbridge, the first director of the port authority, for whom the Outerbridge Crossing is dedicated. It was not until 1981, nearly a century after her death, that she was inducted into the International Tennis Hall of Fame.[440]

IMMIGRANTS, ALE AND INTEGRATION

Throughout the late nineteenth century, immigrants escaping famine and poverty from Ireland, and those fleeing the political consequences of the dissolution of the German Federation, were the dominant groups finding new homes in Richmond County.

The bulk of the Island's German-born inhabitants tended to live around Stapleton, where they were said to "vie with the native Americans in the interest they take in the good government and progress of the community" and had a penchant for "innocent and rational amusements."[441] They established a German Club named *Erheiterung*, German for "amusement," at the corner of Richmond Road (now Van Duzer) and Prospect Street. The "handsome club-house" was the said to be "the largest, most commodious and complete building of the kind, in fitting and furnishing, to be found in Richmond County."[442] It served as the site of countless plays, concerts and large balls.

Along with German people came Germanic culture, and of course, that meant the brewing of beer. Spirits of all types had long been distilled by Staten Islanders, but it was not until these waves of immigrants that the first true commercial breweries popped up. Beer drinkers were eager for Staten Island's ales not simply as a result of the craftsmanship of its brewers but also "on account of the number and copious fullness of the springs and the excellent quality of the water."[443]

Interestingly, the first major operation, the Clifton Brewery, was actually started by the Italian duo of Garibaldi and Meucci in 1851, before its sale to David Meyer and Frederick Bachmann.[444] The immense brewery, now the site of a strip mall on Tompkins Avenue,[445] employed fifty men before its destruction in 1881 by "one of the most disastrous fires ever known on Staten Island."[446]

The Constanz Brewery was founded by August Schmid in 1852 in two small buildings on property along Manor Road opposite Schmidt's Lane. After two decades, it passed into the hands of Monroe Eckstein, a Bavarian-born innovator, who added the latest steam machinery and was able to pump out more than forty thousand barrels of beer each year. Eckstein was a prominent figure in nineteenth-century Richmond County and served as a commissioner of highways, chairman of the Castleton School Board, president of the Richmond County Savings Bank and an executive committee member of the Association of United Lager Beer Brewers of New York.[447]

The partnership of Rubsam and Horrmann gave Staten Island its longest-lasting brewery, first opened in 1870 as the Atlantic Brewery in Stapleton on Boyd Street. Competition between the county's brews was intensely fought, and soon various saloons would boast themselves as "100% R&H" and feature coasters, mugs and signs branded with the trademark R&H logo. Later, the company would be one of the few to survive Prohibition by selling ice and marketing a non-alcoholic beer. In 1953, it sold the business to Brooklyn's Piel Brothers, which kept the plant open until 1963.[448]

By far, the Island's largest brewery was founded in 1853 by a German immigrant named John Bechtel. It passed to his son George in 1865, and it was the younger man who turned Bechtel's Brewery into the county's main producer and the winner of international medals in competitions in Paris and Sydney.[449] As production increased, George built a four-acre site into a rise on present-day Van Duzer Street at Broad Street, "with its connecting buildings, tall and imposing tower, and handsome architectural features, overlooks the village from the top of the hill."[450] It was a commanding structure that "at once attracts the attention and excites the curiosity of every visitor to Stapleton"; with respect to cleanliness, "the greatest care is exercised, not in the brewing alone, but as regards the machinery, floors, barrels, vats, kettles, pumps and other necessary appliances."[451] Like all of Staten Island's famous brews, Bechtel attributed his success at least in part to the Island's aquifer,

COMMISSARY HORRMANN.

August Horrmann was appointed commissary of subsistence for the Eleventh in September, 1879. He has proved fully competent to the duties of his office and has made himself further conspicuous by many personal sacrifices for the benefit of the regiment. Commissary Horrmann is one of the best liked officers in the ranks of our National Guard. He is also popular to an eminent degree among the lovers of good beer, to whom the brewing firm of Rubsam & Horrmann, in which he is a partner, contribute such high-class liquid refreshment.

BREWER ENDS HIS LIFE

August Horrmann Cuts His Throat at a Sanitarium.

Had Been Under Treatment for Melancholia Caused by Illness in His Family.

August Horrmann, the President of the Rubsam & Horrmann Brewing Company of Stapleton, S. I., committed suicide by cutting his throat with a razor shortly after noon yesterday at Dr. Max Wilcke's private sanitarium at 588 West One Hundred and Forty-ninth Street, where he had been under the care of the house physician and a trained nurse for the last two weeks. Up to four weeks ago Mr. Horrmann attended to business daily, and in his actions there was nothing to imply that he con-

August Horrmann was a partner in the successful Rubsam & Horrman Brewery before ending his own life in 1900. *Courtesy of the New York Public Library and New York Times, February 10, 1900.*

which he accessed deep into the side of Grymes Hill. "The water used for brewing is from an artesian well, which is sunk to a depth of 23 feet on the premises and then runs horizontally to the source of supply some 350 yards distant," an advertisement read. "The quality of this water cannot be excelled for brewing purposes anywhere on Staten Island, and the jealousy of not a few other brewers has been excited on this account."[452]

As IRISH IMMIGRANTS SWELLED the Island's Catholic parishes, their welcome to the United States and immigrant experience were somewhat different than those of their German counterparts. For one, Irish immigrants were on the whole generally more destitute than any prior block to enter the harbor; second, they faced a prejudice previously unseen upon landing en masse during the Great Famine. The first generation of Irish on Staten Island would have a hard time developing any business empires like Bechtel or Eckstein.

In 1848, the *Christian Examiner*, a popular periodical, reminded its audience that "the crowds that cross the Atlantic to seek a refuge are in general a ragged contrast to our own well-covered masses" and that "the ill-clad and destitute Irishman is repulsive to our habits and to our tastes."[453] Many who came in this economic condition were also in poor physical health, and so it was the quarantine station in Tompkinsville where they were relegated to spend their first days in this country.

For thousands of predominantly Irish immigrants, the quarantine was sadly where they spent their final days as well, as cholera, yellow fever and typhus took their toll. The dead, as many as 1,500 in a year,[454] were not afforded even a moment of true freedom in the United States and were often buried in mass graves without any record. In the period after Great Famine, the volume was more than officials could bear, and thousands of bodies were stacked and buried two or three deep in trenches at various points on Staten Island.[455] Sadly, only a fraction of the remains have been located.

Although DNA testing on quarantine remains has not been done, it is presumable that a majority of the bodies unearthed over the years were of Irish descent due to the volume of burials done just after the 1848 famine, when Irish immigration outpaced all others. Between 1847 and 1860, the annual reports of the state's Commission on Emigration recorded processing 1,107,034 Irish nationals and 979,575 Germans, accounting for about 80 percent of all of New York's immigrants. At the same time, 88,918 of those entering were held at the quarantine for various ailments.[456]

An 1845 survey of the quarantine grounds shows a small cemetery set just to the rear of the building marked Yellow Fever Hospital, roughly on the present vacant lot next to 100 Central Avenue. This first cemetery was likely used by quarantine employees as early as 1799 and customarily would have contained grave markers to delineate each set of remains. In an amended survey presented to the legislature in 1849, an additional cemetery was marked and in-use at the northwest corner of the property at the present corner of Hyatt Street and Central Avenue, double the size of the original.[457] Clearly during that time, officials saw the need to bury many more bodies than they previously estimated and chose a spot on the gentle rise in the landscape behind the quarantine.

Sadly, the earthly remains at that site would not lie undisturbed. In the early twentieth century, the area of the north cemetery was excavated and developed with private houses. In 1957, when the site was once again cleared for a municipal parking lot, residents recalled seeing the macabre sight of dump trucks filled to the brim with soil and skeletal remains.[458]

As New York City planned this site for a new courthouse in 2000, a formal archaeological survey was completed. The remains of just eighty-three individuals were found by the time it concluded, and they were ceremonially reinterred in vault below a grassy area in front of the building in 2014.[459]

Still, the question of what happened to all of the bodies was not fully answered. Surely, there were far more than eighty-three people buried at the height of Irish immigration after the outbreak of the Great Famine and the before the authorities moved their mortuary operations to Seguine's Point, Hoffman and Swinburne Islands.

Morris's Memorial History of Staten Island, written in 1898, confirms that by that point, Central Avenue had been developed and houses built where once had been the two sites of the quarantine's cemetery. However, he reported that "[t]he bodies buried within these grounds were taken up several years ago, and re-interred in Cooper's Cemetery,"[460] which was the former name of Silver Mount Cemetery on Victory Boulevard.[461] In their 1925 reference guide *Staten Island Gravestone Inscriptions*, historians Charles Leng and William T. Davis transcribed thirty-two tombstones that had been moved. Many of those had English surnames, and that, coupled with the fact that they had formal grave markings at all, suggests that the graves that were reburied were those of the formal south cemetery at the quarantine.[462] Clearly, even if some of the remains from the north cemetery were brought to Cooper's cemetery, many more were left in place to be unintentionally excavated during twentieth-century developments.

Even accounting for both of the quarantine cemeteries that were once on site, it does not end the question of where the bones of the thousands predominately Irish immigrants now rest. In 1849, the state legislature ordered burials prohibited within the immediate surroundings of the quarantine, yet these were some of the busiest years of the Irish exodus and deadliest within the facility's walls. In 1851 alone, there were 1,561 deaths recorded in the Commissioners of Emigration Annual Report, and for the next several years, 10 percent of all those housed at the quarantine would die.[463]

To accommodate them, the authorities bought a new four-acre plot of property one mile from the quarantine along the Richmond Turnpike, opposite Cooper's cemetery.[464] To satisfy concerns that the bodies could cause illness among its neighbors, the burial trenches were set back from the road about five hundred feet. The oddly shaped lot was recorded on an 1874 atlas as the "Marine Cemetery"[465] and similarly on a 1917 edition.[466] It survives today in the same outline as the borough's block 240, lot 1, owned by the Department of Parks and Recreation running behind 937 Victory Boulevard. It now houses maintenance buildings and the eighteenth fairway

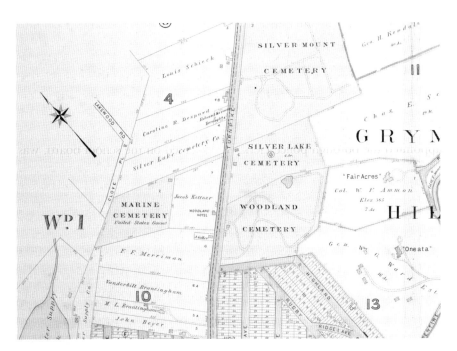

Detail from a 1917 atlas, just over ten years before Silver Lake Golf Course was built, showing the "Marine Cemetery" just set back from the Richmond Turnpike (now Victory Boulevard). *Courtesy of the New York Public Library.*

of Silver Lake Golf Course. A monument to the "Forgotten Burial Ground" was installed there in 2003."[467]

For every Irish immigrant who perished at the quarantine, thousands more disembarked in New York Harbor, swelling the city's poorer quarters and branching their families out into the growing communities of the modern outer-boroughs, including Staten Island. Eventually, those who settled in the county began to have influence on its affairs, and later generations would grow to have an outsized impact. Richmond's civil list between 1866 and the incorporation of 1898 record few Irish surnames.[468] Whereas one or two generations later, its twentieth-century political scene was dominated by Irish Americans, as the Democratic Party and their own "Little Tammany"[469] offered patronage and chance to rise through the ranks. The Italians and their Republican machine came much later.[470]

Perhaps the earliest clear example of this second-generation rise to power is that of Charles McCormack, who became borough president in 1915. Born to Irish immigrants in New York City, he fell under the political wing of Tammany leader and former mayor Hugh J. Grant. As incorporation loomed, he moved to Rossville in 1895, was soon elected assemblyman and sheriff and later was appointed deputy commissioner of water, gas and electric and commissioner of taxes.[471]

William C. Casey was perhaps the only standout Irish immigrant elected to office in Richmond County in the nineteenth century. Born in County Limerick, he journeyed to San Francisco and Chicago before settling in New Brighton for the bulk of his life. In 1882, he was elected a town justice of Castleton, serving two terms; when the county was incorporated, he was appointed the borough police clerk.[472] He served on the school board, was a charter member of the Knights of Columbus, Richmond Council, and a member of the Ancient Order of Hibernians. As noteworthy as his life may have been, it was matched by that of his wife, Mary, whom he married in 1887, in a union that bore eight children.[473] Mrs. Casey, who had a background in nursing, became the first woman in the state of New York to be licensed as an undertaker,[474] and the first Casey Funeral Home was located on the Richmond Turnpike, in Tompkinsville. After William's death and as Mary's age advanced, their fourth son, George, took over the family business,[475] which still survives in two locations.

For most Irish immigrants of the 1800s, however, the struggle to rise above the ranks of laborer proved difficult. Many, though, followed their ambitions to success, and some went on to prosper in the county's real estate industry and construction business. In fact, it was Staten Island's Irish builders, and not speculators from Manhattan, who dominated the home building industry during the mass migration of the late nineteenth century. One such developer was Owen Boylan, who had immigrated in 1880 and began his career working in cooperage shops and shipyards located on Shooters Island, just off the north shore. After a stint with the Baltimore & Ohio Railroad, he organized the Aquehonga Real Estate Company and became its president. When it completed a merger with the Third Ward Savings and Loan Association, his conglomerate became one of the largest land dealing and mortgaging companies in the state of New York.[476] On the construction end, Joseph Johnson and his wife, Elizabeth, left Antrim in 1860 and settled in West New Brighton. He established a contracting firm, specializing in excavations, sewer laying and road building. The business, along with his family, grew ever larger, and by 1882, Joseph Johnson & Sons was capitalizing on the Island's infrastructure expansion from its offices on Broadway. Johnson was an early motorcar enthusiast and a founding member of the Staten Island Driving Club. Sadly, in November 1902, "the well known contractor"[477] was driving his buggy along Canal Street when he attempted to cross the bend in the road in front of the Rubsam & Horrmann Brewery and was struck head-on by a southbound trolley. Johnson was thrown from his mangled carriage and suffered for several days before passing. His funeral made the front-page news, and his fellow driving club members all paid their respects as pallbearers.[478] This was the first fatal automobile accident on Staten Island.

Other immigrants sought an education and professional careers. Dr. Joseph Feeny originally left Sligo for Trinity College in Dublin, where he began teaching. Sensing new opportunities abroad, he came to America and enrolled in the University of the State of New York, College of Physicians and Surgeons. Shortly before his graduation in 1849, he established the Island's first drugstore in Stapleton, revolutionizing the then-established practice of physicians supplying their own pharmaceuticals.[479] His son, Dr. John Feeny, would serve as the health officer for the village of Edgewater and would go on to play a prominent role in the Island's political history during consolidation. Of equal success was I.K. Ambrose, who spent his childhood in Ireland, was educated in France and graduated with a degree in medicine and surgery from Long Island College Hospital in Brooklyn. In the late 1870s, he was affectionately known as the "Irish Doctor," for both the origins of his clientele and the fact that he was the only one of that nationality in the county at the time.[480]

Still other Irish newcomers brought their artistic talents. Captain James Burke, a veteran of the Royal Minister Fusiliers in the Crimean War and the U.S. Marines during the Civil War, was known for his literary talents. In addition to his fifty-one years at the St. George lighthouse depot, he wrote for the *Brooklyn Eagle*; yet it was his poem "Similar" that made him famous.[481] He was offered and refused a spot to write full time for *Harpers Weekly*, preferring instead to remain at the lighthouse. At the time of his passing, he was the oldest living Staten Island Civil War veteran at ninety-two and completed his last poem to commemorate Memorial Day hours before his death.[482]

Beyond all doubt, the most well-known Irish writer to have lived on Staten Island was Jeremiah O'Donovan Rossa, who published *Rossa's Recollections* in 1898 while living in Mariner's Harbor. In it, he described his first impressions of the county, describing "the hills of Staten Island looking as gay and green as the hills of Ireland."[483] Before arriving, he spent time in an English jail for his belief in an independent Ireland and participation in the Irish Republican Brotherhood and Fenian movement.[484] The *Irish World*, New York's leading newspaper among immigrants from the Emerald Isle, called O'Donovan Rossa "the patriarch of Irish revolutionists."[485] He died in New Brighton in 1915, and his body was transported to Glasnevin Cemetery in Dublin. It was by his graveside that Padraig Pearse, a leader of the Easter Rising just months later, gave a rousing eulogy, stirring the hearts of the mourners and commanding them to be "bound together henceforth in brotherly union for the achievement of the freedom of Ireland."[486]

Although Richmond County's nineteenth-century Irish certainly harbored those who espoused revolutionary political beliefs, the Irishman who had the most lasting impact on Staten Island, and whose legacy lasts well into the twenty-first century, was a benevolent priest of humble origins.

Father John Cristopher Drumgoole was born in 1816 in Granard, County Longford. His father died in 1822, and that loss, coupled with a steady decline in Irish agricultural prices, led John and his mother, Bridget, to join the growing waves immigrants entering the United States at the quarantine. For years, he was the small family's chief breadwinner, and due to their finances, he held off fulfilling his calling to become a Catholic priest until he was fifty-three.[487] Upon his ordination, he was assigned to his home parish of St. Mary's, on Grand Street, where he began keeping its basement unlocked at night so that the growing masses of homeless Catholic children could take refuge from the street. Soon, he had taken over a dilapidated shelter on Warren Street that soon became known as "Father John's Home," as he spent his days searching every alleyway and dockyard he could to minister to the city's estimated forty thousand destitute youths.[488]

Father John Drumgoole founded the Mission of the Immaculate Virgin at Mount Loretto as a home to house destitute youth, including the waterfront girls' dormitory building that was demolished after a fire in 2000. *Courtesy of the New York Public Library.*

By 1879, his facility had grown insufficient, but his corporation, the Mission of the Immaculate Virgin, had raised enough money through charitable subscriptions to construct a ten-story dormitory at the corner on Lafayette Street. Yet by the time the building was consecrated, it, too, proved insufficient.[489]

In 1882, Drumgoole purchased more than four hundred acres of beachfront property on the south shore of Staten Island, and by 1885, there were more than seven hundred boys living in its several cottages. The following year, plans were set for a separate girls' facility along the waterfront. Catechism instructions were given for one hour every day, and students were also instructed in Latin, Greek, commerce, carpentry, tailoring, shoemaking, typesetting and gardening. There was a brass band, lectures and a healthy diet of football, baseball and sledding on the property's rolling hills.[490]

By the turn of the century, 2,000 children called Mount Loretto home, and in any year, 200,000 people were served with food, shelter or medical care there.[491] *Donohoe's Magazine*, a Catholic interest magazine, compared the scene to "the loveliest sights in the world."[492] But sadly, Father Drumgoole would not live to see its full success.

In a blizzard that the *Wall Street Daily News* called "an event unparalleled,"[493] Drumgoole attempted to travel from Manhattan to Staten Island and caught pneumonia. He kept his strength for a time but eventually collapsed on his way to morning mass and passed away days later.[494] His wish was to be buried among "his boys," and so he was dutifully interred in a mausoleum on the property at Mount Loretto.[495]

CHAPTER 4

A County Waxes and Wanes

The idea of consolidating New York City with its immediate suburbs had reared its head as far back as the 1830s, when King's County, then organized as any other county in the state with a loose assortment of incorporated villages, applied to the state legislature for a city charter. It is arguable that the power brokers of New York had historically viewed their lesser-developed neighbors as subservient to the needs of their growing city, and it is not a stretch to think they imagined the eventual takeover of the surrounding area as a sort of municipal Manifest Destiny. So, in 1833, when the Assembly passed Brooklyn's new city charter, those Manhattanites who opposed the measure were able to thwart its momentum in the State Senate. The following year, when the bill was reintroduced, the opposition from their neighbor resumed, but this time the city's Common Council issued a legislative report arguing for that New York's annexation of King's County because, as it argued, separate governments were stifling development on both sides of the East River. For good measure, the council added Richmond County into the potential conglomeration as well. These efforts only delayed the inevitable, however, as the charter passed the legislature and was signed into law by Governor William Marcy in 1834. The city of Brooklyn was born.[496]

Brooklyn's charter put off the inescapability of total consolidation for nearly sixty years. There would, however, be sporadic inklings of it, as the legislature passed bills like the Metropolitan Police Act of 1857, consolidating police in the counties of New York, Kings, Richmond and Westchester into the "Metropolitan police district" under a commission with members from each county.[497] Additional bills set up similar systems for the fire and health departments and created a common system of regulating excise duties. Each of these would remain in effect until the so-called Tweed Charter of 1870, wherein members of the Tweed ring, known for their rampant corruption, were able to wrestle control away from state authorized commissions and back into the local control of the city, where they held the purse strings.[498] Again, Richmond County was simply caught in the mix.

By the time the idea of consolidation of the city and its neighbors returned, Brooklyn had grown into the country's second-largest city. There was a real need for cooperation on efforts to bridge—in a literal sense—the East River, as the cost was staggering and the existing ferries overwhelmed. Yet if there was a clear argument as to why New York and Brooklyn should be linked into an urban giant, it remained to be seen why it would ever include Richmond. Moreover, the very man who was leading the consolidation effort, Andrew Haswell Green, was the same man who chaired the 1870 legislative commission that highlighted the poor conditions and numerous problems of developing Staten Island. What value could he see the outlying county adding to the new metropolis? Conversely, what benefits could the inhabitants of Richmond County gain through consolidation?

Green had never held elective office, instead catapulting himself through a succession of successful bureaucratic and philanthropic roles. He had been the driving force behind the creation of Central Park, a reformer who had taken on Tammany Hall and one of the few comptrollers in that period who did not use the post to enrich himself. By the 1880s, he was one of the most prominent public figures in the city, with a reputation for honesty and foresight. But beyond his ideas on what physical characteristics the modern city should take, Green also believed that centralization was a prerequisite to any successful urban plan and a necessity of the city's ever-expanding municipal bureaucracy. As he struggled to develop Central Park, he realized that duplicative governments at the county and city level, multiple public authorities with overlapping jurisdiction and two separate but powerful political powerbases in Brooklyn and New York City Halls would stifle growth throughout the city's metropolitan region.[499] It is likely that part of the reason Green eagerly chaired the 1870 Staten Island Improvement Commission was to gauge its suitability for inclusion in the new metropolis, which he termed "Greater New York." Despite the troublesome report, the urgent need for incredibly expensive infrastructure and the seemingly poor opinions of the commissioners, Richmond County eventually made the cut when Green finalized his plan.

The commission's report did nothing to bolster the public perception of Staten Island, though, which reached a low point in the late nineteenth century. *Harper's New Monthly Magazine*, one of the most popular publications, took a haughty and unfavorable view of the county, despite the fact that one of the Island's most prominent residents, George W. Curtis, was the magazine's political editor. In an article entitled "A Spring Jaunt on Staten Island," it wrote, tongue-in-cheek:

> *Staten Island is one of the unloveliest, unhealthiest, and least romantic of haunts….It is a reservoir of Teutonic beer, a scattering of uninhabitable villas, a humid nursery of mosquitoes, and its exhalations are blue with pestilential chills.…We might as well make the tour of a back yard as Staten Island.*[500]

But in spite of its poorly developed infrastructure and abysmal public perception, conditions on the Island were not as bad as they seemed. Richmond was a little empire, complete with industries, institutions and effective governments. There was enough prosperity, it seemed, that the monied interests and do-good reformers of Manhattan had an interest in bringing it into the new city. Still, the county was well on its way to its own independent prosperity, with or without casting its lot in with its neighbors.

Institutions Old and New, Good and Bad

By the time its residents voted to support consolidation in 1894, Richmond County was home to a number of institutions that served Staten Island's own needy population as well as the wants of the poor from New York City. Even before Father Drumgoole brought his street children, others saw the Island as a potential for respite and recovery for those requiring it. In fact, the Children's Aid Society—his Protestant "competitors," as some may have seen it during an era of tension between "natives" and immigrants—had already been housing destitute children from Manhattan in the county for many years. That organization was founded in 1853 by Protestant philanthropists and reformers led by Charles Loring Brace, a Calvinist minister and close friend of Frederick Law Olmsted.[501] It purchased a large tract in New Brighton, formerly the estate of Charles Goodhue, containing ample woodlands and a brook.[502] An 1874 magazine illustration shows dozens of children, swinging from the trees, strolling the grounds and feasting in the dining hall, far removed from the tumultuous streets city.[503]

For other children who resided on Staten Island, the Young Men's Christian Association provided a welcome distraction and ample activities from an otherwise tough life on the county's farms or in its Industrial Revolution factories. The YMCA was formed in England on the premise that Christian men of all denominations should have places to bond and develop moral standards

A magazine depiction of children playing at the Children's Aid Society on Staten Island in 1874. *Courtesy of the New York Public Library.*

while enjoying newly popularized recreational pursuits.[504] The North Shore YMCA was organized by the Trinity Methodist Episcopal Church in 1867. It soon acquired a large building on Richmond Terrace for $20,000, with a sizable library of one thousand volumes and a 450-seat auditorium where it hosted lectures, soirees and debates. The YMCA opened a second chapter with a larger gymnasium in 1883 through the Brighton Heights Reformed Church on the site of modern Tompkinsville Park.[505]

There were countless other smaller charitable institutions that supported any number of causes and misfortunate neighbors. The directories of the 1880s and 1890s list dozens, mostly located on the north shore. West New Brighton was home to an industrial school and the Nursery and Child's Hospital, while Clifton had St. Mary's Orphan Asylum. Just to its north, the German Mutual Benevolent Association had its home, as did the Old Ladies' Society of Stapleton. There was the Father Mathew Total Abstinence and Benevolent Society of New Brighton, as well as St. John's Guild for poor children across the Island in New Dorp.[506] Both St. Peter's and St. Rose's parishes hosted a chapter of the Young Men's Catholic Union, and *Der Deutsche Frauen Verein*, the German Women's Society, held its monthly meetings in Germania Hall in Tompkinsville. By 1900, one also had the choice of joining the Society for the Prevention of Crime, the Sons of Liberty, the Needlework Guild of America or the county's chapter of the Society for the Prevention of Cruelty to Animals.[507]

The institution that would go on to become Staten Island University Hospital also traced its origins to this period. It was not, however, the first or only healthcare facility on the Island. There was, of course, the quarantine, as well as the Marine Hospital and Eye and Ear Hospital in Tompkinsville;

the Nursery and Child's Hospital; and the Sea Side Hospital for children, operated by St. John's Guild.[508] However, Staten Island Hospital is the longest in continual use and was available to any person in the county affected by trauma or disease.[509]

The hospital dates back to 1861, when members of the Richmond County Medical Society operated a small infirmary on the corner of Bay Street in Stapleton for "the care of the sick, poor, and for the reception of casualties."[510] Its first formal hospital opened in 1869 in a renovated building on the original quarantine site. The organization incorporated that year as the S.R. Smith Infirmary and bears the distinction of being the first private, nonprofit hospital in the county.[511]

Over the next two decades, the institution raised significant sums from the philanthropy of prominent Islanders like the Vanderbilt, Bechtel and Jewett families. In 1887, Dr. George Frost donated six acres of land along Castleton Avenue, where by 1889 the iconic S.R. Smith Infirmary building was built, with its imposing castellated and turreted design.[512] The name Staten Island Hospital wasn't adopted until 1917, but sadly, the original "castle" building was demolished in 2011.[513]

Two other notable institutions date back far earlier than consolidation and were flourishing by the time it came about. Both are intrinsically linked, but only one would be embroiled in a headline-dominating scandal at the end of the century that had ramifications in Staten Island's political circles and in the debate for consolidation itself.

In 1846, several upper-caste New Yorkers organized a foundation to care for the destitute children of seamen who worked around the harbor's thriving maritime industry.[514] The institution briefly resided in a small home in Port Richmond before operating in Stapleton until 1852. That year, a large facility was erected at Sailors' Snug Harbor, then itself more than twenty-

A postcard depicting the S.R. Smith Infirmary Building, an iconic structure that served as the precursor to Staten Island University Hospital. *Courtesy of the New York Public Library.*

Postcards depicting Snug Harbor's buildings at the turn of the century. The sanitarium, as well as the domed Randall Memorial Chapel, was destroyed in the 1950s. *Courtesy of the New York Public Library.*

one years old, which could accommodate about one hundred children on five acres of the property at its south end, along Castleton Avenue. There it would remain for seventy-three years.[515]

Its landlord, Sailors' Snug Harbor, had been in concept since the 1801 death of Robert Richard Randall. He had been a wealthy merchant, the son of a lucrative French and Indian War privateer, and was both well connected and well intentioned. In his will, drafted by Alexander Hamilton,[516] he bequeathed his Manhattan farm toward the purpose of creating an "Asylum" to "maintaining aged, decrepit, and worn-out sailors."[517] It was not until 1831, after years of lawsuits, that his trustees began work on a 130-acre farm they purchased on the north shore of Staten Island. In 1833, Sailors' Snug Harbor opened its original imposing building with its noteworthy Greek Ionic octastyle portico for its first thirty-seven retired seamen.[518]

By the late nineteenth century, several more buildings had been erected. A large dorm was completed in 1880, and a memorial statue to Randal was placed in a prominent position.[519] Snug Harbor residents ate three meals a day in one of four "well appointed and well lighted" dining halls and were issued "two full suits of clothing, made to measure," each year.[520] The entry requirements were "a sea service of five years under the United States flag, and a physical condition that makes the applicant incapable of self-substance." Records indicate the average age for admission was fifty-four, death at sixty-four,[521] and as the men lived out their final years, they were greeted each day with decorative signs on the walls with comforting sayings like "Rest, after Dangerous Toil" and "Port, after Stormy Seas."[522] However, unlike the placid messages that lined the halls, all was not copacetic at the sailor's retreat.

The Snug Ring

The late nineteenth century saw a host of bitter fights between the notoriously corrupt Tammany Hall Democrats and reformers like Sam Tilden, Republicans like Theodore Roosevelt and even a cartoonist named Thomas Nast. The battle for the political control of New York City played a critical role in the storyline that led to the city's eventual consolidation, and while Tammany conflicts in Manhattan take center stage in that tale, Staten Island was not without its own corruption scandal, which occurred at, of all places, Snug Harbor. Supporters of consolidation like Andrew Haswell Green had long argued that the proposed larger metropolis was the only true antidote to Tammany's corrupt control over New York City.[523] And for many Staten Islanders, the likelihood that the machine was already taking hold was validated by the events at Snug Harbor.

In the 1890s, "Boss" Nicholas Muller was, in title, the chairman of Richmond County's Democratic Party and one of the county's upstanding police commissioners. More importantly, he was the Staten Island ally of the grand sachem of Tammany Hall, Boss Croker, and the "bulldozing" leader of what the *New York Herald* called the "Snug Machine."[524]

Muller was a German immigrant, a former state legislator and congressman from Lower Manhattan. In the late 1880s,[525] perhaps with the encouragement of Croker, he moved his family to a stately home in New Brighton from where he orchestrated his takeover of the Staten Island Democratic Party. His tactics were hardnosed. He didn't hesitate to kick Republican poll watchers out of polling sites or use other bare-knuckle tactics when he could. The *Herald* noted that he was "dominating the political affairs of Staten Island" with a machine that "out-Tammanies the Tammany methods."[526]

The Democratic Party's use of Snug Harbor to assist in voter fraud predated Muller's tenure, but the issue boiled over under his watch in 1889. That year, the sailors' retreat was run by Captain G.D.S. Trask, who was appointed governor by the board of trustees and rumored to harbor Republican views.

At first, news broke that twelve retired sailors were expelled in what was presumed to be some sort of political retribution. The *Herald*, eager for sensational front pages, billed Trask as a "czar" under the headline "No Room for Democrats at Sailors' Snug Harbor."[527] On their way out, the alleged victims claimed that their treatment was "fuller of terrors than Russia."[528] The story told of Gus Hyland, "a cripple," who was seemingly expelled for being a member of the Democratic County organization and who worked the polls during the county's local elections weeks earlier, in a year the Snug Harbor poll site near unanimously voted for the Democratic ticket. The article mentioned several other men, all "broken down salts" and members of the Muller's Democratic Committee, who after a two-month-long investigation by Governor Trask were "turned into the street in a single day."[529]

The backlash against Trask was swift. Political leaders, trustees and reporters all swarmed the gates of Snug, demanding to inspect the claims of oppression and mistreatment as reported by the *Herald*. The residents they spoke to did not dissuade the fact-finders that Trask had been anything other than a partisan tyrant, bent on cruelty. They demanded the trustees of Snug Harbor investigate, and they obliged.[530]

The start of the inquiry did not soften any of animosity toward Trask, nor did it satisfy the personal vendettas of the twelve Democrats kicked out to the curb. One of them took matters into his own hands. On December 7, 1889, six months after his eviction, Captain E.P. Anderson attacked Governor Trask as he tried to leave the waterfront railroad station, just below the campus. A scuffle ensued, as both men rolled down the stairs on to the train platform. Anderson managed to fire three shots from a revolver at fairly close range. One bullet found its mark, but in a case of ironic fate, it was stopped by a folded copy of the *New York Herald* in Trask's jacket pocket, the very newspaper that had been unwavering in its criticism of him. Anderson showed no remorse for the attempted murder and instead only muttered his apology to the arresting officers for failing to finish the job.[531]

Trask's luck continued. The board of trustees, comprising some of the leading political figures in the city, decided in 1890 to readmit several of the men who had been expelled.[532] They also had to decide who would lead the institution going forward in the face of public outcry against the "cruel" and "autocratic" governor.[533] However, after the board's lengthy investigation, it ultimately decided in favor of Governor Trask. All but one trustee voted to reelect him. Moreover, they entered into the record endorsements of his official conduct and added vindicating statements on the prevalence of election fraud. "For twenty-five years or more…Snug Harbor had been an open market for the buying and selling votes at the local, State and National elections."[534] The following month, in front of a grand jury, prosecutors showed evidence that of the 572 sailors residing at the Harbor, "243 of those inmates not only took money for voting, but would not vote unless paid to do so, and that this custom had extended over several years."[535]

Logic would dictate that the 1890 scandal and subsequent investigation would cause the "Snug Machine" to slow down, yet instead, the Democratic Committee and its cronies would not reach the peak of their debauchery until 1893 and 1894. By then, Nick Muller had full control, and the scandals and depredations intensified.

Finally, though, Muller and his ring began to lose some political battles. The sale of votes at Sailors' Snug Harbor during the 1893 elections occurred in plain sight, and the county's elected officials had finally had enough. The following June, several poll inspectors from the town of Castleton were sentenced to thirty days in jail and ordered to pay at $250 fine.[536] By October 1894, thirteen more of Staten Island's Democratic operatives from Southfield, Middletown and Castleton had been sent to the penitentiary. The most severe sentence fell on James Hewitt, a poll inspector from the Castleton's Ninth District encompassing Snug Harbor, who spent a year in prison.[537] Most severe, just days to go before the 1894 election, a county judge ruled that the residents of Snug Harbor would not be permitted to vote.[538]

The scandal went far outside the walls of Snug Harbor and exposed the Muller Ring for what it was: an extension of Tammany. The county police force, directly under his control, was also implicated in the ring and for covering up election abuses. The *Staten Island Independent* alleged that the police force had played a role in reporting inaccurate counts and that it likely was involved in collecting political intelligence for Muller and the ring.[539] As the election of 1894 loomed, the motivation to vote out members of the Muller gang became conflated with the broader desire to use consolidation vote to rid the county of Tammany and all its allies. As the *Independent* editorialized, "The people are more than ever motivated to root out Mullerism and boss domination from every branch of local government. Determination is stronger and confidence is greater than ever before."[540] The exposé of the Snug ring had deep political consequences.

This is not to say, however, that the Snug scandal would lead to a consensus on consolidation. While the editorial pages of the *Staten Island Independent* argued in favor of its passage, claiming that it could eliminate countless patronage offices, the currency of the Tammany Ring,[541] other Richmond County residents strongly disagreed and did not hesitate to let the *Independent* know it. Charles Sanders, a Port Richmond bicycle dealer, declared just the opposite, saying, "Politicians advocate consolidation because it will create nice political plums," and that "Staten Island... should not be used as a prop to a thoroughly rotten municipality."[542] These concerns of workaday Staten Islanders that Tammany-style corruption and machine politics could infect their county were not without merit, but even Sanders had to admit that "it could not make the county much worse than it was under the rule of Nick Muller."[543]

THE TITANS OF STATEN ISLAND

One of the principal reasons for consolidation, according to its advocates, was that it would guarantee commercial growth in each of the five new boroughs. Real estate development was the top concern, and Green's 1870 Improvement Commission clearly had land speculation on its mind when it compared the Island to similar developing suburban counties around the country as well as the transit improvements then pushing the sprawl in London and Chicago.[544] In fact, the Windy City had succeeded in the largest suburban annexation in its history just a year before Green's report.[545] Richmond's newspapers saw the same potential, and as consolidation seemed likely, they gleefully reported on how "vast schemes for development" of Staten Island were "now under way."[546] But as Chicago was going on to annex even more of its surroundings in 1889, adding a whopping 133 square miles and thousands more people,[547] New York's propertied interests were only just beginning to organize.

While Chicago grew, the New York Chamber of Commerce and the *Real Estate Record and Builders' Guide*, the mouthpiece of the city's real estate industry, pushed for the type of centralization and urban planning that would boost local properties.[548] The 1880s saw an unprecedented growth in the city's housing market, averaging three thousand new buildings each year and with land values surging 50 percent. New row houses stretched far up Manhattan's east and west sides, and developers were simply hungry for more.[549]

New York's business community had other concerns too. How could New York possibly remain competitive against Chicago if it surpassed its population? The 1890 census showed it trailing with just 1.1 million people to the 1.5 million on Manhattan.[550] Even closer, Philadelphia consolidated in 1854, instantly quadrupling its population.[551] In 1890, that city also surpassed 1 million people.[552] The prevailing belief, as evidenced by a number of pro-consolidation pamphlets of the day, was that if New York were overtaken by Chicago or anywhere else, it would lose "its commercial prestige and standing as chief city of America" and squander "business, music, society, politics, the drama, everything."[553] In sum, the instantaneous population growth that annexing its neighbors would bring New York City would result in the continued prestige of being the country's largest city, and that prestige would generate continued commercial growth.

However, the need for population could not totally address why Green, the chamber of commerce and other pro-consolidation capitalists eventually included Richmond into Greater New York. In 1890, its population stood at 51,000, a mere drop compared to Brooklyn's 900,000.[554] If an increase of people and of buildable lots were the only drivers, advocates would have been fine by simply annexing Brooklyn. Between that city and the portions of southern Westchester that had already been annexed to New York in the 1870s and 1890s (the future Bronx), there was room for decades' worth of new housing developments.

Instead, the need for Staten Island centered on its waterfront. As afraid as New York may have been to be surpassed by Chicago, industrialists feared that the inefficiencies of the port system around New York Harbor, governed by multiple local governments, was rendering it less desirable than

Turning the Island's bucolic turn-of-the-century waterfronts, like this one in Mariner's Harbor, into more robust ports was the goal of many consolidation supporters on Staten Island and around the new city. *Courtesy of the New York Public Library.*

New Orleans, Boston, Baltimore and Philadelphia.[555] Their fears were not unfounded, as the 1880s and 1890s saw a relative decline of the port's market share, as decaying wharfs, poor support roads and limited rail networks sent shipping lines elsewhere.

There was nothing preventing port growth or improvements under the pre-consolidation government, and it is true that there had long been cooperation on labor and economic interests across the harbor. Brooklyn workers of all classes, from lawyers to laborers, had always relied on the business opportunities and markets of its larger neighbor to sustain its economy.[556] In many ways, it was the country's first bedroom community, with Staten Island following shortly behind. On the other side, Manhattanites saw prosperity across the East River along Brooklyn's waterfront, over which the city had long maintained a sort of political fiefdom, dating back to the Dutch. Its wealthy residents had industrialized, financed and paid taxes on Brooklyn businesses and land, despite not formally residing there. As Green put it, "The water front of Long Island, from Astoria to Bay Ridge, is largely owned, developed, built upon, and used by New York merchants—the docks are frequented by ships, the warehouses filled with merchandise by their order."[557] For the chamber of commerce crowd, they simply wanted more control of the waterfront, both politically and financially.

It was this desire more than any other, certainly more than any altruistic desire to make improvements for the people of Richmond County, that caused the geographic boundaries of the consolidation effort to encompass all of the land of lower New York State with frontage on the harbor. The decision to include enough of Queens County (the "unnecessary" part became Nassau) to secure Little Neck Bay in the north and Jamaica Bay in the south was done so with future bulkhead in mind. Likewise, the purpose of adding Staten Island was more or less a power grab on its nearly forty miles of coastline.[558]

Delving a bit deeper—or rather, looking deeper inland—Green also made it clear why he and consolidationists valued the comparatively vacant portions of Staten Island, Brooklyn and Queens. Ports were only as valuable as the commodities they traded, and the open land could provide space for vast factories, homes for new workers and transit infrastructure to move goods and people. Green believed, rather presciently, that the port would not attract foreign commerce simply by the fact that it had a well-situated natural harbor, but rather because it had the most regional goods available for export on its own docks and the most extensive domestic distribution network. As he informed the state legislature in 1890, "Newport, in our near vicinity, has a fine a harbor as our own, and Norfolk a better, yet they are but little else than summer watering places."[559] Ships came calling in New York because of what its factories could produce, and New York's economy rested on the $126 million in wages earned by hundreds of thousands of workers.[560] Green and his allies saw the potential of Staten Island's waterfront, its thriving factories and the brand-new rail bridge connecting it to the New Jersey mainland. The county's recent successes and the space available to expand industry and infrastructure made it highly desirable.

As the century progressed, Richmond County succeeded in expanding its industrial base. Breweries would no longer have the only smokestack darkening its skies.

Many of the companies that began operating were already depending on a thriving port to sustain their business. The county did not produce any cotton, for example, but in 1872, the American Dock and Trust Company warehoused cotton and exported it to overseas clients from its facility in Tompkinsville,[561] covering the ground now called Bay Street Landing.[562] Its president, Alonzo B. Pouch, went on to form the Pouch Terminal Corporation on Edgewater Street in Clifton, another logistics outfit, and at the time of his death, he was regarded as "the most important man in civic life on Staten Island."[563]

To service port operations, Richmond's shipbuilders transitioned into primarily repairs and retrofits. The Island's lack of renewable timber posed a problem for the newer and larger ships of the day. The north shore had three large shipyards to boast, but the bulk were located on the south shore along the Arthur Kill and serviced about five hundred vessels per year. The Tottenville docks thrived on repairs from the frequent needs of oystermen and a steady clientele of New Jersey coal barges.[564]

In 1874, the American Linoleum Manufacturing Company developed a two-hundred-acre property at the western end of the Richmond Turnpike, where it produced linseed oil–based flooring. The area, once known as the New Blazing Star Ferry, now Travis, was then called Linoleumville in homage to the factory town that sprang up.[565] Its British inventor, Frederick Walton, and his local partner, Joseph Wild, were the first to manufacture the popular affordable product in the United States.[566]

The fabric dyeing industry had a home in the county dating back to the 1819 formation of the New York Dying and Printing Establishment. It was one of the first factories in Factoryville, and according to historian Richard Bayles, there was no other industry outside of oysters that had been more associated with the name of Staten Island.[567] The company

WORKS OF THE N. Y. DYING AND PRINTING EST. ON STATEN ISLAND.
OFFICES, 45 JOHN-STREET, and 720 BROADWAY, N.Y.

New York Dying and Printing Establishment was one of the first manufacturers in Factoryville when it formed in 1819. *Courtesy of the New York Public Library.*

occupied a site nearly three blocks long and required the construction of massive factory lake, the bottom of which is now home to Alaska, Warren and Chappell Streets.[568] At its height, the company had fourteen offices and one thousand agents over a territory that stretched to the Mississippi. In 1850, a breakaway employee opened his own factory just a mile away along present-day Forest Avenue near Barrett Avenue,[569] and with the launch of Barrett, Nephews, & Company, Staten Island was home to two of the largest commercial dyeing operations in the country. As nationwide demand grew, Barrett was forced to expand to three hundred new workers along Post Avenue,[570] and in 1881, a third outfit, the Irving Manufacturing Company, opened its doors on Jersey Street for the production of "linings, tarlatans, plushes, etc."[571]

Balthasar Kreischer was born in Bavaria in 1813 to a family who had long manufactured bricks. After hearing of the great fire of 1835, which destroyed seventeen blocks of Manhattan's business district,[572] he immigrated to New York to take advantage of the incessant pace of brick reconstruction that followed. His original brickworks were located along Delancey Street, which, despite its size, was unable to keep up with the demand. Kreischer began purchasing land in the town of Westfield, in a small hamlet called Androvetteville, which had ample deposits of kaolin clay.[573] The factory town that resulted was thus an odd outcome of a fire on Hannover Square.[574]

Despite its distance from the city, Westfield had some of the highest land values in the county in the 1840s and '50s, and Kreischer's acquisitions around Androvetteville proceeded slowly. The land value wasn't a result of the clay, but rather its soil. As the *Mirror* explained, "Their farms are of small extent, but are highly cultivated and enriched with a prodigality of fruit trees, and their neat white-washed cottages, many of which were built by the

French Huguenots…are held by the descendants of the original owners."[575] The locals who farmed this land for generations were also not necessarily keen selling to New York land speculators. "We don't want any '*forners* [foreigners] coming in here to meddle in our politics," said one "worthy islander" of Androvetteville to the *Mirror*.[576] Still, Kreischer proceeded, and an 1853[577] map and 1874 atlas shows that what was once a scattering of houses turned into a proper village, including churches, stores, a school and a post office. The name was also formally changed to Kreischerville[578] and later Charleston.

The atlas also records two small rail lines: one transporting bricks from the factory to a storage area and another to remove the clay from a marked pit to a waterfront dock about a mile away. The latter became Ellis Road.[579] The Kreischer properties where the kaolin clay was harvested was later preserved as Clay Pit Pond State Park Preserve.

The other lasting feature of the neighborhood is the landmarked Kreischer Mansion, standing on a promontory above Arthur Kill Road. This house, however, was not the house where Balthasar Kreischer resided. His Italianate villa was built in the 1860s farther inland, resting on a hill with a commanding view of his factory and docks. The house that still stands was one of a pair of near identical homes built for his sons, Charles and Edward, around the time of Balthasar's death in 1886.[580] Edward's house was destroyed by fire in the 1930s, but he was not alive to see it. In 1894, the "cheerful" and "popular" gentleman, an upstanding philanthropist and church, walked about one hundred feet south of the brickworks to a small wooded creek named Drake's Spring, now buried under the Tides of Charleston senior residences. There, he raised a gun to his head and pulled the trigger. A local boy who worked at the factory found him slumped over on his face, blood pouring out of his temple.[581]

The Kreischer legacy would long outlast the family's presence in Charleston. The three-acre brickworks and terra cotta factory are long demolished.[582] Yet many of the buildings still remain. The houses along Kresicher Street built by Peter Androvette to house factory workers were designated landmarks in the 1990s, as was the school at 4210 Arthur Kill Road, originally called the Westfield Township School No. 7 in 1896. Balthasar Kreischer was also responsible for the construction of the St. Peter's German Evangelical Reformed Church of Kreischerville, now the Free Magyar Reformed Church, on Winant Street, built in 1883 to accommodate the ecclesiastical needs of his German workforce. It was landmarked in 1994.[583]

By the late nineteenth century, the Kreischers, along with the Pouches and others, had become part of an industrialist class that found itself in concurrent roles as board members of Staten Island's institutions, dabblers in county politics and financiers of vast commercial enterprises. The Jewett family was another example. One member owned the Jewett White Lead Company in Port Richmond, employing one hundred people.[584] Another founded the Unitarian Church of Staten Island and served as a village trustee, while another Jewett directed the North Shore Ferry Company.[585] Still another helped found the Cricket Club.[586]

Other businessmen were less focused on local matters, but like other Staten Islanders, they were concerned about their ability to ship via the county's new rail link or through the expansion of its ports. They saw consolidation as a benefit. This was the case with the S.S. White Dental Manufacturing Company, which by the 1890s had become the largest employer in the county, with 425 workers operating out of its "factory by the sea" on Seguine's Point. By the 1920s, a postwar boom saw it become the largest dental manufacturer in the world.[587]

Seguine's Point had been a hub of industry throughout the nineteenth century. The Seguine family had been living on Staten Island in the vicinity of Prince's bay since at latest 1706,[588] and its most prominent nineteenth century member, Joseph H., was a part of numerous civic and commercial endeavors. It was he who built the large white antebellum residence still standing today. The family's second-most prominent member was arguably Anna Seguine, the wife of Stephen Seguine, an officer of the Staten Island Railroad.[589] When it came time to name a station near the 160 acres her family owned, it became Annadale.[590]

Around 1860, both Joseph and Stephen Seguine built a factory on Seguine's Point. At first, they extracted plant oil, but when it proved fruitless, they shifted to manufacturing candles. In 1865, when that business failed as well, the partners sold the site to the Johnston brothers, who began the dental business. After merging with S.S. White, they would continue to manufacture dental instruments on that property until 1971.[591]

Several similar factories would thrive well into the twentieth century. For example, the Unexcelled Manufacturing Company began manufacturing fireworks and other explosive novelties in Graniteville in 1887. The factory went from employing twenty workers in four buildings to more than two hundred employees in 167 buildings by 1930.[592]

Other companies peaked in the nineteenth century and did not survive long after, although consolidation wasn't the cause. The International

Ultramarine Works at the waterfront of Johnson Street in Rossville manufactured a royal blue dye it called ultramarine, which they extracted from the nearby clay pits.[593] It also had a light rail line that transported the clay from its source to a waterfront factory.[594] The company was started by a group of German chemists in 1884, and when the United States entered the First World War, the government confiscated the property under the Alien Property Act. It had determined that its largest shareholder resided in Cologne, Germany, and that the total "enemy interest" was 100 percent.[595] It valued the company at $255,000,[596] and the property eventually become the Industrial Loop manufacturing area.

Other companies also fell off due to events far beyond their control. The ice industry, which at its peak employed several hundred in five harvesting companies, was rendered extinct by the advent of refrigeration. The first icehouse was built in 1835 at Clove Lake, then called Britton's Mill Pond. The last burned to the ground in 1920. At the turn of the century, no pond was spared, including Silver Lake, Brady's Pond, Factory Pond, Martling Pond and Brook's Pond. Each icehouse was typically constructed as a large barn with two layers of exterior walls three feet apart, with the gap stuffed with sawdust and hay, which could insulate the ice efficiently enough that only 30 percent would melt over a year.[597]

Clearly, Staten Island had an outsized share of industry for a county with just over fifty thousand people. Its geographic location and abundant waterfront helped, as did its access to capital from New York. Small manufacturers thrived too, and they would have certainly looked at consolidation as an opportunity to ship their wares beyond the county limits. One glance at the *Richmond County Advance* on the eve of consolidation shows a wide array of small factories and dealers. There was, for example, James Thompson, "dealer of all kinds of lumber and timber,"[598] who shipped his goods from Broadway in West Brighton. Nearby stood the concern of R. Lemmer & Company, "manufacturers of carriages and light wagons," as well as the New York House on the corner of Bond Street and Jewett Avenue, which imported wines, liquors and cigars "for family and medical use."[599]

As consolidation was weighed, there was no shortage of local businessman, large and small, who saw only the opportunity to come. This group formed the crux of Richmond's pro-unification faction, and they were the ones who smiled brightest when people like Andrew Haswell Green promised the infrastructure improvements to come with consolidation. In his view, Staten Island "will require but a few years to render her an indispensable auxiliary to the growing business of the port," as "the only portion of our territory situate upon the west side of the harbor, with an ample bridge connecting her with the main shore, and a tunnel projected to perfect communications with Brooklyn, with best docking facilities for sea traders of all the ports." To him, "the future of Staten Island is assured beyond all hazard.[600]

The Structure of Staten Island

One of the arguments repeatedly used to justify consolidation was that the new mega-city could muster financial resources on a scale never before seen, much of which would benefit Richmond County. Its role in Greater New York would be significant, and an honest and benevolent government would bestow its share of its riches with its southernmost subdivision. Many merchants bought into this, like R.G. Tompkins, a clothier, who believed that consolidation would bring "a number of improvements without raising our tax rate," including new ferries and wider roads.[601]

Others didn't buy it and instead believed that Richmond's own government might be best to maximize its own future potential. Levingston Snedeker, whom the *Independent* described as a "young real estate man," cited all the promises of consolidation—better roads, fire protection, public works and a reduction in taxes—but then asked, "If a municipal government is desired, would it not be just as beneficial to our own welfare to incorporate Richmond County as a city?"[602]

Mr. A. Greenwald, "the dry goods man," was more poignant and even prophetic:

> *Many of the inhabitants of our island believe that by consolidation with New York City our beautiful island would transformed into a paradise....I hope some day to see our city shield raised and the national flag flying from our own city hall. What do we gain by consolidation?...We will lose our identity, and be but a minority in the governing boards of Greater New York.*[603]

Of course, Staten Island did already have a substantial government. In many ways, and ignoring the morality of Nick Muller, it is fair to assume it was neither failing nor shortchanging its constituents. There had even been efforts to incorporate the Island's towns under one unified and well-run county administration.

Public education was just one area where the county demonstrated an ability to govern. Public schools had been a priority for the state for decades, and it was Staten Island's own Daniel Tompkins who used his 1810 inaugural address as governor to commit to permanent funding for public education. Seventy-five years later, his home county's school system was robust, educating 7,200 students, about half of those eligible. The schools were broken down in to five districts, one for each town, and enrollment ranged from Middletown's School No. 2 in Stapleton, with 1,284 children, to 50 in New Dorp's tiny Southfield School No. 3.[604] As the historians Leng and Davis claimed, the majority of these districts were run successfully and economically, boasting a household tax for education at just thirty-five cents in 1885.[605]

These districts were not necessarily independent. A law requiring an elected countywide school commissioner took effect in 1856, and along with a board of three trustees from each district, a county body controlled the finances of all schools. On the eve of consolidation, the commission received $23,345 from the state and raised $123,200 through county taxes.[606]

In addition to its public schools, the county government made attempts to improve higher education that, unfortunately, did not prove equally fruitful. There were efforts to form a Richmond county college as far back as 1838, when an act of the legislature granted its charter. After several tries to acquire property, "the matter finally died away and was forgotten."[607] The Island would not house a college until the twentieth century.

There was success, however, in the formation of libraries. Beginning in 1845, county school records make references to "library money" from the state to form small libraries in each school. But for the most part, the libraries of nineteenth-century Staten Island were privately held collections. Just before the Civil War, there were reading rooms in New Brighton, Stapleton and Tompkinsville, all privately owned. In the 1880s, two formal reference libraries were also established by the Staten Island Institute of Arts and Sciences and the Staten Island Academy.[608] In 1894, two St. George residents tried to form a subscription-based library, offering two rates: for five dollars annually, you could borrow one book every two weeks; for ten dollars, they were delivered.[609] The venture didn't take off. Free public libraries were organized just after consolidation and constructed through the largess of Andrew Carnegie between 1899 and 1909 in Tottenville, St. George, Stapleton and Port Richmond.[610]

The county was also working to address the more rudimentary needs of its residents. The Island's water table, which had long been prized by Richmond's brewers, began piping into houses along the north shore by the Staten Island Water Supply Company in the 1880s. The company pumped its water, described by a chemist as "clear and odorless," from a series of wells near New Brighton to a reservoir atop Fort Hill, from where it was sent downhill to residents.[611] Construction was slow, but at the turn of the century, the company supplied 5,600 customers and 656 fire hydrants from its 750,000-gallon reservoir.[612] By then, four separate companies were providing water service. The Crystal Water Company, formed in 1883, was the second-largest operation, servicing 3,300 customers.[613] Its iron-rich water, once been believed to cure rheumatism,[614] was taken from a source called Mineral Spring in Winant's Swap and was one of the springs that lead to naming the area New Springville.[615]

By consolidation, the Island also boasted a modern electrical grid, not far behind Manhattan's. Electricity was first brought in to power the linoleum factory in 1882, which by coincidence is now the site of the county's only power plant. Three years later, George Bechtel electrified his brewery, his home and greenhouses. Wiman built the first power plant to supply his amusements at St. George and Erastina. Eventually, he sold it to the Edison Electric Illuminating Company, which lit the streets of Edgewater and New Brighton in 1888. A second plant was built on Davis Avenue in West New Brighton, and both merged into the New York and Staten Island Electric Company in 1897, operating throughout the Island.[616]

While infrastructure was coming together, in terms of political subdivisions, the Island was coming apart. By midcentury, the county contained five townships: Northfield, Southfield, Westfield, Castleton and Middletown, its latest addition. In 1866, mimicking other counties in the state, Richmond further fractured into a number of additional village municipalities. The villages of Edgewater, Port Richmond and New Brighton were chartered on March 22, April 24 and April 26, respectively.[617] These were essentially political constructs, with their lines drawn irrespective of the legal boundaries of each township and the de facto boundaries of housing clusters. Edgewater, for example, occupied parts of both Middletown and Southfield and encompassed the neighborhoods of Clifton and Stapleton but only parts of Tompkinsville.[618]

Each village charter was amended frequently as wards were added and removed. New Brighton initially had four wards, but in 1872, the entire town of Castleton was included, giving the village two more; whereas in 1876, Edgewater changed from having nine wards to just two before settling on five in 1884.[619] The charter of New Brighton was amended by the state legislature five times in seven years.[620] This system was as confusing then as it is now, especially so in Edgewater, where the village name was hardly used.

Residents preferred to use the names that had long been associated with steamboat landings (like Stapleton, Clifton and Tompkinsville). Even an 1886 guidebook quipped, "There is no post-office called Edgewater, and in fact in the matter of villages, government, post-offices, towns and steamboat landings, things are all mixed up throughout Richmond County."[621]

Despite confusion and limited functionality, other neighborhoods sought a charter. Tottenville endeavored to form a village in 1862, but the state rejected the proposal.[622] In 1894, a charter was granted, allowing the small town of 2,500 to begin levying the $35,000 to macadamize its main thoroughfares.[623] Yet with consolidation looming, the incorporated village of Tottenville lasted but five years.

Richmond County also professionalized its police force. After the Civil War, the Island was served by town constables and supplemented by private policemen hired by the villages.[624] By then, deeper problems associated with the corruption of the New York City Municipal Police had led Albany Republicans to push through legislation in 1857 phasing out that department and replacing it with the Metropolitan Police District. Wrestling the department and its patronage appointments from the Tammany machine was the number one priority, and broadening its governing body would prevent it from infecting the new system.

This department was overseen by a board of commissioners appointed from each county, and it had jurisdiction in New York, Kings, Westchester and Richmond. It took years to implement, and the legislature amended the law in 1860 to add several towns in Queens County as well. In 1866, the legislature approved funding for Richmond County to employ one captain, two sergeants and twenty-five men, much fewer than the 2,000 allocated for New York or the 368 for the city of Brooklyn.[625]

The system was far from perfect and largely unwelcome by Staten Island's elected officials, who were significantly outnumbered when it came to its governance. From the outset, the county refused to pay the $335.32 it was assessed,[626] despite a clear sentiment in the city that the Metropolitan Police system was far more preferable to the old municipal force. As the *Times* opined, "A comparison of the existing Police Department with that of ten years ago will readily convince any skeptic that the change was wisely made....[E]very man of the force being appointed by a central board that knows no man's political or religious opinions, and cares not what they may be."[627]

Still, Staten Island likely did not see the need for the reform in the first place. Self-governance was far more important, and in 1870, a change

The Metropolitan Police Department was expanded to include a contingent for Richmond County in 1866, becoming one of the first forms of consolidated municipal government. Here, its members show their uniforms. *Courtesy of the New York Public Library.*

was welcomed. Richmond still refused to pay its share and faced a lawsuit from police commissioners. But separately, Tammany Hall managed to win enough elections to take back total control of the city and promptly passed the "Tweed Charter," a New York City charter that effectively returned expanded home rule to the municipality. The reorganization and decentralization of the police force came with it, meaning New York would once again have a Tammany-controlled force and Staten Island would have its own.[628]

The legislature created the Richmond County Police force in 1870, and its manual the following year mimicked the anti-corruption rules of the previous Metropolitan Department. It banned the practice of holding a second job and prohibited all "gratuity, rewards, or gift, directly or indirectly."[629] John Laforge was named its first captain. The governing board consisted of three commissioners appointed by the county judge and the five town supervisors and operated largely scandal-free until Boss Muller brought his Tammany tactics to the board upon his appointment.[630]

Richmond County Police had two stations in the 1880s and '90s: Station 1, located at 19 Beach Street in Stapleton, and Station 2, along Richmond Terrace in West New Brighton. Both were connected by telegraph to terminals in Richmond, Rossville, Kreischerville and Tottenville, ensuring that a force could quickly be dispatched in an emergency. The 1886 guidebook described the force of fifty men as "a body of able, intelligent and worthy men who always do their duty," and that "altogether the men are favorites with the people."[631]

Richmond County did not, however, feel the same way about its fire service. Certainly, there was pride in its companies and appreciation from the citizenry. However, unlike the efforts to retain control of the police force from outside entities, Richmond County was looking toward consolidation to bring better fire protection. In fact, the entire future city was hoping that the merge would result in better service because, as one pro-consolidation pamphlet put it, "Inadequate fire department apparatus causes immense conflagrations, and no money can be had to buy first class machinery."[632] On Staten Island, this sentiment was summed up by Reverend Leonard of Port Richmond's Park Baptist Church: "We would have…better means of fighting fires, although our volunteer department is very efficient and deserving of the highest praise."[633] The *Richmond County Advance* was much harsher, criticizing the North Shore Fire Department for its handling of an 1891 emergency by citing its "utter inability" to provide "protection from the ravages of fire."[634] This prompted a sharp response from the department's secretary, who quickly blamed the neighboring Edgewater Fire Department and its Tompkinsville Hose and Engine Company for bungling the job. Although he claimed that the "paid fire department of any city could not have saved that fire box," the mere accusations of antagonism between companies, rather than cooperation, surely confirmed the need for better organization.[635] Throughout the nineteenth century, the problem of rival fire companies fighting one another—sometimes literally—to be the first on scene, or allowing political and neighborhood rivalries to fester among their ranks, was not unique to Staten Island. It was common practice in New York and all of the major urban areas of the country.[636]

Richmond County was long protected by these volunteer companies, dating back nearly seventy-five years to the first mention of a "fire company at Factoryville" in 1828. Soon they were joined by others: the Cataract Steam Engine Company (1844), Washington Engine Company (1853), New Brighton Engine Company (1856), Enterprise Hook & Ladder Company (1856), Port Richmond Steam Engine Company (1859), Clifton Engine Company (1863), Clifton Hose Company (1863) and at least a half dozen others.[637]

After the Civil War, and following the lead of New York City, the county tried to organize its sporadic collection fire companies into two better-organized and better-functioning units, the North Shore Fire Department and the Edgewater Fire Department. Outside of these two, single companies still operated, such as the Oceanic Hook and Ladder in Travis, organized in 1880, and the Richmond Hook and Ladder Company in 1895.[638] Tottenville had also organized two of its own companies by 1886. The Protection Hook and Ladder was housed on Washington Street (now Arthur Kill Road near Main Street) and had forty-eight volunteer members who met on the second and fourth Tuesdays of each month. The Eureka Engine Company No. 2

The "Last Call" of the volunteer Medora Hook and Ladder Company before its replacement with a professional city company, Ladder 79, on Castleton Avenue. The photo may show the building in its original design, before its renovation and rededication as part of the FDNY in 1905. *Courtesy of the New York Public Library.*

was housed at the present-day corner of Butler and Craig Avenues and had forty-six members. They met on the first Wednesdays.[639]

Certain private companies and factories also maintained apparatuses and trained their employees in their use. The linoleum works were one example. Unfortunately, this did not always work out, and when the Consolidated Fireworks Factory in Graniteville went up in flames in 1895, predictable results followed. As sparks flew, the factory's owner even thought it best to prevent the local fire company from entering the grounds and instead trusted the work entirely to his own company men and their pumps. After a half hour battling the flames, the entire building was destroyed.[640]

The professional company that was barred from the Consolidated Fireworks fire was likely a part of the North Shore Fire Department. The nearby Granite Engine was part of its ranks.[641] By 1888, the North Shore Fire Department was made up of four engines, four hook and ladders and four hose companies. This agency was noted for its professionalism, and local insurance companies even charged lower rates for homes within its jurisdiction.[642]

The Edgewater Fire Department, the larger and older of the two, was chartered in 1871 and consolidated the existing units within the town, including the Tompkinsville company, the Clifton companies and Enterprise Hook and Ladder.[643] Within fifteen years, the department consisted of five engines, two hook and ladders, four hose companies and two bucket brigades. The *Illustrated Sketch Book of Staten Island* claimed that "few localities are so fortunate" to have fire protection of this caliber in 1886.[644]

Yet despite many of the positive aspects on living on Staten Island in the late 1880s—including its municipal services, the development of its factories and infrastructure and the ongoing work of its charitable institutions—it would be only a few short years before its residents would vote to reorganize its fire and police services, and nearly everything else for that matter, under the city of Greater New York. The rationale for consolidation may have been treated as a mixed bag for many Richmond County residents, but it fell on its politicians to sell the proposal. Their efforts would prove as equally disjointed as the rationale for doing so in the first place.

CHAPTER 5

The Politics of Greater New York

T he parade stepped off from Elm Park just after noon on a clear autumn Thursday after months of intense planning by the Island's leading citizens. The buildings along the route were "gayly dressed,"[645] Chinese lanterns lined the streets and shops and schools were closed to mark the occasion. A platoon of six mounted policemen led the procession, the queue extending four miles to its rear, all marching along to the Stapleton waterfront, where the USS *Vidalia* stood at anchor ready to unload its twenty-one-gun salute. "Upwards of two hundred of the heavy broad-backed brewery horses" were "used to draw the cannon, cars, and trucks."[646] The full pageantry of Staten Island was on display, and a line of march was recorded by the *New York Herald* to include "barouches laden with dignitaries, brass bands, posts of the Grand Army, fire engines and their companies; more brass bands; flower laden chariots, in which were emblematic maidens and mock savages; wagons of tradespeople and brass bands. The Goddess of Liberty, a young woman well known on Staten Island, was greatly admired for her flowing locks of reddish blonde tint."[647]

This parade marked an important historical milestone—not for the nation's centennial or to mark the anniversary of evacuation day. It was November 1, 1883, and Staten Island was celebrating its bicentennial, two hundred years after it was established as Richmond County under Governor Thomas Dongan. With fantastic pomp, the citizens of Staten Island were boastfully displaying their civic pride in residing in one of New York State's longest self-governing subdivisions. Only a small number of counties in the country could claim such a lengthy pedigree. As speakers took the stage under the two grand tents, one by one they spoke of Richmond's unique and independent history. Erastus Brooks cited Henry Hudson and his remark that the Island was "the best land for tillage on which he ever set foot."[648] George W. Curtis struck right at the heart of the crowd. He observed how his community has often resisted the type of change that occurred elsewhere, teasing, "If Rip Van Winkle had awakened from his long nap on Staten Island instead of in the Kaaterskills," he would have said, "It's the same old place."[649]

Curtis continued, prophesizing the county's future:

> *Here lies our Island…the "pleasantest and most commodiousest" site in all the land, and to-day our beating and answering hearts are the promises that the genius of that spirit is opening its eyes and about to put forth its hand, which shall bring the Island still nearer to the great city, shall reclaim all its waste and watery spaces, shall fill its air with the hum of cheerful industry, and shall justify to every Staten Islander the promises that the beauty of our Island holds to every passer by, and to every stranger who lands upon our shores.…God shall stimulate this county, shall make the county what it long ago should have been, in Shakespeare's verse, "This precious stone set in the silver sea. The most resplendent jewel of th' imperial crown," of the most imperial Commonwealth of New York.[650]*

The pride Staten Islanders felt that day as an independent county would never be on display again. Despite all the sentiments, it would be less than a decade before Staten Islanders began the process to formally lose their identity, and eleven years later, almost to the day, Richmond's citizenry would overwhelmingly vote to abolish their county government and self-determination. Political change came fast and hard.

TYSEN'S FOLLY

During the 1880s, Andrew Haswell Green was preoccupied with binding New York City with its neighbors physically, if not politically. He had served on the original commission for the Brooklyn Bridge and pushed the construction of a bridge across the Harlem River in 1886. Over the next few years, he focused on erecting a second bridge across that waterway for railroad service.

But while Green remains the undisputed "Father of Greater New York," it fell on the others to keep the dream of consolidation alive. Just after the Bronx's annexation, a collection of Brooklyn's property owners, developers and businessmen formed the Municipal Union Society of the City of Brooklyn and the County of Kings. This organization sought to unify Brooklyn, the five neighboring towns in Kings County and New York City. Years later, the powerful New York Chamber of Commerce took up the cause and likely gave it its most potent push. In 1887, the organization essentially started the political process by urging the state legislature to consolidate the cities of New York and Brooklyn.[651]

Andrew H. Green is widely considered the "Father of Greater New York." He was murdered in 1903 in a case of mistaken identity. *Courtesy of the New York Public Library.*

The chamber also met with Mayor Abram Hewitt and convinced him that the only way to finance the infrastructure needed to expand port operations was to coordinate the efforts of the harbor under one government. In his annual message in 1888, the mayor made it clear that New York must be partnered with Brooklyn and connected by road and rail through Harlem to the newly annexed Bronx if it hoped to keep its port competitive. Months later, the chamber issued its annual report, reiterating the need for transit improvements and suggested consolidation as the simplest avenue for implementation. The *Real Estate Record and Builders' Guide* followed suit shortly thereafter.[652]

Noticeably missing in all of the discussions of 1887 and 1888 were Andrew Haswell Green and Richmond County. That would soon change.

David J. Tysen II was born in New Dorp in 1841, on the lane that still bears the family name. His ancestors were original Dutch settlers and received a small grant of land on what was then called Karle's Neck in New Springville. By David's generation, they had moved their homesteads to New Dorp, and it was he who began purchasing tracts farther south from the Guyon family. He was a lawyer by training but became what Leng and Davis called the Island's "oldest real estate developer" after purchasing large farms and subdividing them into various rental properties. He also went on to build an agricultural empire of tomatoes, corn and squash, all of which was grown on his farms, canned in his canneries and shipped to Manhattan. In the 1870s, he purchased the last remaining iron mines on Todt Hill Road and Jewett Avenue, from which he exported about 120,000 tons to the Bethlehem Steel Company. Tysen was also active in Republican and reform politics. He was nominated for the New York legislature and Congress but declined both; he even turned down an ambassadorship to a fledgling South American republic. Among his friends he counted Ulysses Grant, Benjamin Harrison, Teddy Roosevelt, Seth Low and Chauncey Depew.[653]

In his memoirs, Tysen recalled learning about the growing movement to consolidate New York's harbor counties through newspaper accounts, which at the time were likely coverage of Hewitt's speeches and the chamber of commerce's report. Incensed that Staten Island was left out of the efforts by Brooklyn's aristocracy and New York's civic leaders, he decided to call on his acquaintance Andrew Haswell Green, whom he first met while working with another Staten Islander, Frederick law Olmsted, on the plan for Central Park.

Writing more than a quarter century after their meeting, although he does not give its precise date, we have only Tysen's words to go on.[654] He paid a visit to Green at his office on Broadway in Manhattan. He found him alongside Colonel George Waring, a former a former Union cavalry officer and later the new city's street commissioner who was feted for cleaning up the streets of New York.[655] Green at once showed Tysen a proposed map of Greater New York, of which he claims to have remarked, "You've left out the best part!" Waring responded, "Ha Ha, Staten Island is too far down the Bay....About fifty years hence, when you have much larger population, and much fewer mosquitoes you may consistently ask to be included in the City."[656] No doubt Waring, who had been working with Green on draining the swamps of Central Park at the time of the Staten Island Improvement Commission, was familiar with its assessment.

Nonetheless, the colonel left the room, and Tysen and Green conversed over the advantages of including Staten Island. Green said he had "food for thought" and intended to go over the matter with the small coalition that was beginning to form to support the effort. He urged Tysen to call on him again in a few days, and when he did, the Staten Islander was pleased to see a new map of Greater New York, this time including Richmond County.[657]

By 1889, Andrew Haswell Green was fully re-engaged in the effort to consolidate Greater New York; when, at his urging, a bill was introduced in legislature to further the effort, Staten Island was included.[658]

The Battle for Albany

The bill that was introduced in the state legislature in 1889 was not an outright consolidation bill. Instead, it authorized a commission to study the annexation of the proposed areas by the City of New York. That year, it was sponsored by Assemblyman Ernest H. Crosby, Theodore Roosevelt's Republican successor from Manhattan's Twenty-First District and chairman of the Assembly's important Cities Committee.[659]

The bill met unexpectedly heavy resistance from Manhattan's uptown real estate families, believing that the new city's attention would be focused on the infrastructure of Brooklyn and not on pushing development north. While within Brooklyn's limits, there was strong opposition from politicians allied with Tammany Hall. These two groups found a spokesman in the newly elected mayor Hugh J. Grant, an uptown developer and Tammany stalwart, who lobbied strongly for its defeat.[660]

At this point, not all of Richmond County shared the pro-consolidation opinion of David Tysen either. In politics, Staten Island had become substantially aligned with the Democratic Party following a brief surge in Republicanism after the Civil War. The 1870s saw veteran and mechanic John G. Vaughn ascend to the chairmanship of the county Democratic organization. Historians Leng and Davis wrote glowingly of Vaughn, calling him a "man of clear vision" who "avoided personal aggrandizement."[661] They cited the candidates he put up for office as a basis for why the party grew so quickly, a fact easy to see when one examines the careers of politicians and statesmen like Erastus Brooks.[662]

Public perception of the county's Democratic organization dramatically altered with the coming of his successor, Nicholas Muller, but at the time of consolidation, the county was still governed by Democrats and sent a Democratic delegation to Albany. Only one out of the five town supervisors was a Republican, earning Abraham Cole of Westfield the affectionate nickname "Lone Star."[663] On the issue of consolidation, the Democrats in office were equally as unexcited as their counterparts in. Nathaniel Marsh of Southfield—chairman of the board of supervisors and, at least in title, the head of Staten Island's government—questioned whether taxes would rise and how the county would struggle to keep its voice in an amalgamated municipality. He informed the press that no member of the board was prepared to support consolidation at that time.[664]

Not only were Democratic supervisors on the fence at that point, but so too were many prominent politically active citizens. The *New York Herald* reported,

"Staten Islanders as a general thing are seemingly not as enthusiastic over the proposed annexation of their pretty island under Mr. Green's scheme as they might be."[665] Leading the list in opposition was Erastus Wiman, who ironically was at the same time a leading voice for the annexation of his native Canada by the United States.[666] He called the idea of joining New York "sentimental" and cautioned against the Island "being made the tail end of a great place. Better let it remain as it is, independent, to look after its own interests."[667] He continued, "Take Port Richmond, for example. It does not owe a dollar, has magnificent roads, a fine water supply…and the taxes are low."[668] What benefit could it attain by taking on the liability of the city's immense debt to finance a comparatively worse municipal government? Wiman was echoed by E.H. Outerbridge, who declared, "We are not ripe yet to come into the city" and lamented its lack of benefits, while R. Penn Smith, a real estate developer, griped, "We are fairly well off as we are, and to come into the city could only place unremunerative burdens on our shoulders."[669]

These arguments mimicked similar ones concurrently being made in Long Island City,[670] Westchester County (which was eventually left out)[671] and, of course, in Brooklyn.[672]

Crosby's bill was debated in the Assembly on April 4, 1889, making the fault lines plain to see. Brooklyn's delegation argued strongly against consolidation, and all of its twelve assemblymen pledged to vote against it.[673] Nonetheless it was approved by the committee and then the Assembly and then transmitted to the Senate. In the end, it was the combination of Brooklyn's senators siding with those taking their direction from Tammany Hall and Mayor Grant that sealed its losing fate that year.[674]

In 1890, Green, the chamber of commerce and their allies came back to Albany more determined. This time, Green brought his most comprehensive study of the benefits consolidation would bring to Greater New York. In what has been described as a summary of his administrative philosophy, he laid out, in minute detail, each problem the region faced, from its trouble coordinating maritime efforts to the lack of honest government, and explained how a consolidated government could resolve them. It explained to the legislature how the new municipality could capitalize on modern technologies and finance projects to develop the greater city in a comprehensive vision.[675] With the Brooklyn Bridge not yet a decade old yet transporting a 250,000 people per day, it was easy for legislators to comprehend the need to finance additional large-scale projects.[676] As urban historian Barry J. Kaplan summarized, it "completed the intellectual rationale for consolidation…and for a union that transcended local or parochial interests."[677] The argument quickly won the support of the State Assembly, where a bill introduced by Manhattan Republican Frederick Gibbs passed by the overwhelmingly Republican majority.[678]

Green's other tactical change in 1890 was to hire an energetic lobbyist to work the legislature and the editorial boards of major newspapers.[679] The public perception of the lobbying business in the nineteenth century was equal to the poor reputation it has today. However, its effectiveness was never in doubt. The *Herald* called them "cunning" and confessed that they "had the benefit of extensive experience";[680] one legislator confessed to the *Tribune* in 1885 that they "have more knowledge of the state of legislation than any other men in Albany."[681] The method proved fruitful, and before the Senate began debating the bill, five newspapers came out in support.[682] The Republicans controlled the majority, and the bill moved swiftly through the Senate. The Tammany legislators and their allies from Brooklyn put up some resistance, but the bill passed.[683] In 1890, Staten Island formed a minority portion of the Fifth Senate District, which included a large swath of Lower Manhattan. Its shared Democratic senator, William L. Brown, was co-publisher of the *New York Daily News*, a paper that did not support consolidation. He voted alongside the New York Tammany men against the bill.[684] There was one final skirmish as the Senate attempted to confirm the commission's nominees, as Brooklyn's delegation fought to its last breath. The attempt was unsuccessful, and on May 8,[685] Governor David Hill signed the bill and announced the appointment of Andrew H. Green and five others to the commission.[686]

The first big hurdle had been overcome, and the speculation on what was to come began. That Sunday, the *Herald* ran a feature entitled "Behold New York The Greater," including a large sketch that imaginatively portrayed what the new city would look like in 1950. The paper dreamed that the future metropolis would be one of rapid transit and bridges, and the picture showed no fewer than twelve bridges spanning the East and Harlem Rivers, four connecting Manhattan with New Jersey, three joining Staten Island with New Jersey and one large structure with an elevated roadway spanning the Narrows between Staten Island and Brooklyn.[687]

THE PEOPLE DECIDE

Pursuant to the legislation, the Municipal Consolidation Inquiry Commission consisted of the mayors of New York and Brooklyn; the heads of the boards of supervisors of Long Island, Westchester and Richmond; and several other important citizens. George J. Greenfield represented Staten Island, and of course, Andrew Green served as its chairman.[688] Within months, however, it became clear that there was a fracture among its members and that this was just the beginning of a very long struggle. Green had hoped to push through a full consolidation bill in the 1891 session of the legislature and believed that he could convince all involved to quickly adopt a newly chartered city with a strong centralized government. By the second meeting, he had become well aware that his fellow commissioners were not entirely on board.[689] Greenfield stood in solidarity with the delegation from Kings and Queens to defeat Green's proposals, which they felt would rush the process without the "fullest and freest discussions."[690] The commission did send a bill to Albany that year, and it did manage to pass the Senate. However, the fault lines that formed among the commissioners were essentially replicated in the Assembly, where the bill died through opposition from Westchester, Kings, Queens and Richmond County members. Its death blow rested on there being yet no public support for consolidation in many of the areas slated for inclusion.[691]

Over the next three years, consolidation bills presented at each annual legislative session gradually became weaker, as it became clear that a public referendum must to be a part of the process.[692] Even Brooklyn's strongest proponent, and perhaps Green's closest ally on the commission, J.T. Stranahan, agreed. Citing "more favor than [he] anticipated" from his home city, he told the commission, "The whole matter is one for the people to determine for themselves. The opponents of the scheme are principally outlying towns, which do not want to give up their identity."[693] Many of Brooklyn's prominent citizens mimicked Stranahan's demand for a popular vote, believing that a majority of that city would favor the effort. In 1892, there were efforts to force commitments from all of Kings County legislators to support, at the very least, a public referendum.[694]

As Stranahan claimed, some opposition to consolidation in 1892 and 1893 came from "outlying towns" concerned about their identity. That included Richmond County, a comparatively small island on the periphery of the harbor. Although some of Richmond's elite began warming to the idea, they likely did not yet represent a majority. Erastus Wiman, for example, neutral on the subject two years earlier, now informed the commission that there was "no higher duty" than promoting consolidation. Like many, self-interest may have been a motivator, as he hoped to develop low-cost housing for the new city's "vast mass of the industrial population," who had "no hope for a home northward," where "accommodation is afforded for residences of the better class."[695]

The concept of losing local identity did certainly play a factor in the minds of Staten Islanders. The county's representative on the commission, George Greenfield, former counsel for the village of Edgewater,[696] submitted a proposal in 1893 that existing villages must be represented in any new municipal government. In essence, he hoped that towns would still have a role and survive with some power in the new charter.[697]

Many others openly expressed their doubts on other facets, including George Curtis. He informed the commission that Richmond County would be supportive of consolidation if an effective case could be made that "it would lessen the taxes and give us better roads, cheaper water and a better police and fire department."[698]

After the commission spent three unsuccessful years attempting to get a public referendum bill on a specific charter, the one that finally passed in 1894 included little more than the requirement that a public vote be held.[699] A charter bill would have to wait until after the referendum—a fact that would benefit pro-consolidation forces, as the vagueness and lack of specificity of the future government could theoretically meet every need and avoid every problem. Green, an elitist himself, was never a major proponent for a referendum in the first place; he viewed it as mere pandering. Yet the vote affected his part in the process in a dramatic way. As the focus now shifted toward persuading regular citizens, rather than legislators and commissioners, he was no longer at the helm of the consolidation movement.[700] He would never truly dig himself out of this diminished role throughout the rest of the process.

The debate to convince the public began well before the referendum bill passed—almost as soon as the demands for such a vote had begun. It was assumed that Manhattanites would approve the measure with a substantial margin and that Brooklyn would be the true swing district. To engage those voters, the Brooklyn Consolidation League formed in 1893 as a formal organization for pro-consolidation forces. As the most well funded, they soon proved to be the voice of the movement in every county, publishing some 2 million pamphlets in the lead-up to the vote.[701]

The most important pamphlet was "How Taxes in Brooklyn Can Be Reduced by One-Half" by attorney Edward C. Graves. It would eventually be read in every precinct in the proposed city, but in 1893, agents of the Consolidation League handed a copy to each and every person exiting the Brooklyn Bureau of Taxes and Assessments.[702] Graves's sequel, "Greater

New York. Reasons Why," was written in early 1894 for a broader audience and argued that Richmond County was always historically linked to, and somewhat under the jurisdiction of, the city of New York.[703] From what we can derive from the arguments, it seems as though Staten Islanders were more interested in the taxation argument than by any assertion of New York's dominance over the county.

For example, when George Greenfield leveled his final appeal to the electors of Richmond County, just days before the vote, the title of his letter to the editor published in the *Staten Island Independent* was "Greater New York. How Consolidation Would Decrease Our Taxes."[704] In it, he borrowed Graves's argument that New York's capacity to issue bonds will lower property taxes, concluding that in the scale of the Greater City, Richmond's debts would be "a mere bagatelle."[705]

By 1894, all seemed to be going well for pro-consolidation partisans. Most of the major New York newspapers had come out in favor of the cause, including the *Herald, Tribune, World, Sun* and *Times*. A Consolidation League canvass of several districts in Kings County showed 64 percent of voters in favor of the merge.[706] Even the *Richmond County Advance*, which was opposed, was forced to admit in February that there was a "growing sentiment in favor of the scheme here on Staten Island."[707]

Things progressed smoothly, and it appeared that consolidation would pass easily. Then came the State Senate's Lexow Committee hearings in the middle of 1894, throwing a Tammany wrench into the process.[708]

That committee, named after its chairman, was tasked with investigating Tammany's police corruption in New York City. Weeks turned into months, as witness after witness exposed how the department extorted business owners, took bribes, demanded protection money and brutalized those who refused to comply.[709] Each day, headlines ran highlighting the corruption of Tammany and New York's cops. On one day in June, the *Tribune* ran three stories: hush money to a captain to ignore a brothel,[710] a bribed witness[711] and the Tammany-allied governor accused of attempting to scuttle the committee.[712] The impact on consolidation was clear. Residents of the proposed city questioned the prudence of tying their lots to such an unethical system.

Brooklyn's largest and most staunchly anti-consolidation paper, the *Brooklyn Eagle*, scoffed at the idea of merging with its corruption-plagued neighbor in a series of short editorials. "Brooklyn is a city of Homes and Churches. New York is a city of Tammany Hall and Crime government....Government here is by public opinion and for the public interest. If tied to New York, Brooklyn would be a Tammany suburb, to be kicked, looted, and bossed as such."[713]

On Staten Island, the threat of Tammany was an even more tangible fear than in Brooklyn. Recall, this all occurred at the same time as the investigations of the Muller Ring, resulting in indictments at Snug Harbor and exposing the corruption of Richmond's own police force. The crimes of Staten Island's Democratic machine were so egregious that even the *Tribune* admitted that "nothing the Lexow Committee has brought out in this investigation of the affairs of New-York is too horrible to apply to the methods of government by the ring on Staten Island."[714] When the *Richmond County Advance* opined against the referendum, it was this concern that topped its list. It feared for the future of Staten Island should it become "the tail-end of a big Tammany kite."[715]

To combat this view, the Consolidation League pushed further that the new municipal government would be better suited to rid itself of Tammany's hold. Graves's second pamphlet claimed that Greater New York would be "so large that no Ring or Hall can possibly control it."[716] Albert Shaw, a prominent academic and journalist, believed that the scale of at-large elections in the new city would be such that it would allow for only "representatives of the best elements of business life" and noted that in London, where consolidation had created its own mega-city, there "were no saloon keepers or ward bosses" in its new municipal government.[717]

How would average Staten Islanders view the situation? Would they accept that a new city could rid Tammany's hold on them, or did they believe it would usher a new golden age of machine corruption? Certainly, some newspapers believed the former. The same day the *Staten Island Independent* called for all Islanders to support consolidation, it ran denunciations of Muller and claimed that a vote for the Democratic slate would equal voting to "perpetuate ring rule and boss domination."[718] The *Tribune* did the same, urging support for consolidation and "for honesty against corruption" by electing candidates opposed to Muller.[719]

The Lexow Committee didn't dampen the hopes of consolidation, and as Election Day loomed, the fervor picked up. Commissioner Greenfield led the debate on the Island, promising cheaper transportation, lower taxes, better government and a greater say in the new city.[720] Looking back, the *Independent* would give him credit for having the largest influence on shaping public sentiment,[721] although he didn't act alone. Other prominent Staten Islanders were equally prolific in pushing its merits, including Reverend John C. Eccleston, who preached at the St. John's Episcopal Church in Rosebank.[722] From the bench, Judge Charles L. Benedict pushed consolidation too. The Dongan Hills resident was the first judge appointed to the newly created Eastern District of New York by Abraham Lincoln in 1865, where he served for more than thirty years.[723] Local politicians also spoke up, including Assemblyman Daniel T. Cornell, president of the village of Edgewater, and Charles E. Griffith, the treasurer of Port Richmond.[724] They were joined by Livingston Satterlee, a retired Civil War general and an active member of the New York State Chamber of Commerce,[725] and Captain Jacob Houseman, a "prominent banker and oysterman."[726] David Tysen, who after confessing in his memoirs that he faced anxiety over the result of the referendum, took an active part in the effort and recalled that he and the others "made a lively canvass."[727]

The Consolidation League's efforts and those of its allies on Staten Island proved fruitful. On November 6, citizens throughout the conglomeration of counties, cities, towns and villages voted overwhelmingly in favor to consolidate into Greater New York by a final vote count of 176,530 to 131,706. In Brooklyn, where animosity toward the new plan was most ingrained, the measure passed with a razor-thin 277 votes.[728] Yet it was Richmond County, farthest away from the new city hall and least physically connected to its new confederates, that provided the clearest affirmation of consolidation: 5,531 Staten Islanders voted in favor, while only 1,505 voted against it. With 80 percent, the "yes" vote was substantially higher in the county than the 57 percent garnered citywide.[729] Additionally, the results indicated that the measure had wide bipartisan support; the 3,799-vote margin was significantly higher than that for both Republican governor Morton and Democratic congressman Franklin Bartlett.[730] The other significant outcome was that the Muller Ring was handily defeated in an election that was described as "one of the quietest that has ever been known."[731] In a clean sweep of the county-wide offices, the candidates endorsed by the Republican Party and an anti-Muller reform faction of Democrats won for assembly, sheriff and coroner.[732]

LEGISLATION AND LEVERAGE

The referendum's result confirmed the public desire to see consolidation through; however, it still needed legislation to finalize the merger and form a new charter. The outcome also took many by surprise, especially much of the well-to-do set in Brooklyn. Soon after, they organized the Loyal League to try to kill its momentum or at least slow its progress. The political fight was not nearly over.

As the consolidation debate raged, the Loyal League commissioned songs and held banquets to sway momentum against the plan. *Courtesy of the New York Public Library.*

Within months of the election, the Loyal League boasted a membership of almost double that of the Consolidation League and a full fifteen thousand more than voted against the measure itself. That year, the coalition of Loyal Leaguers and its legislative allies proved to be powerful enough to block charter bills introduced at the behest of Governor Morton.[733]

The year 1895 saw Green partially sidelined and a new leader emerge to direct and carry out the plan, albeit with a different motive. The defeat of Muller and his Democratic machine in Richmond was not unique. As it turned out, the 1894 election gave the Republican Party its greatest resurgence in years and solidified its control of the state legislature. Leading the New York Republicans, and thus pulling strings throughout all of New York State, was the so-called easy boss, Thomas E. Platt, who quickly took interest in seeing consolidation through.[734]

Platt served three nonconsecutive terms in the U.S. Senate between 1881 and 1909. In 1887, he ascended to his powerful position as chairman of the New York State Republican Party.[735] As boss, it is easy to understand his rationale for supporting consolidation. He hoped that a larger city that included Republican-friendly Brooklyn could finally wrest control from of Tammany Hall and that perhaps a candidate under his control could even swoop up its first mayoralty. Additionally, given the requirement that the new charter and nearly every piece of legislation affecting the new city go through Albany, Platt believed that he could be the undisputed string-puller of the state. As such, he shut his eyes and ears to any criticism and began to ram consolidation through the legislature in 1896.[736] The fight took on a new and decidedly anti-Tammany tone.

As Republicans tried entrenching themselves in the Albany legislature, so, too, did their Staten Island counterparts try to build on the success they saw at the 1894 polls. As soon as the new crop took office, they attempted, through legislation, to remove Muller as police commissioner by requiring the position be filled by popular vote.[737]

Republicans and reform Democrats also sought to eradicate the Muller Ring's power in the Richmond County's local offices in the elections that spring. Edward P. Doyle, a vocal anti-Muller Democrat and candidate for Northfield supervisor, took out a large ad in the *Independent* denouncing the Democratic boss and telling Staten Islanders, "I was not controlled by the leader of my party when his power was absolute and I am not likely to be managed now."[738] He went on to squeak out a victory by 115 votes. In fact, the entire election of 1895 was a rout of Nick Muller and his cronies. The *Independent* squawked the headline "Only One Muller Man Left," as only one of the five town supervisors, Dr. John Feeny of Middletown, son of the famous immigrant doctor, was a ring crony.[739] Republicans were elected in Castleton and Westfield, and Nathaniel Marsh, a Democrat whose candidacy was opposed by Muller, won Southfield by 40 votes.[740] Later that year, the village of New Brighton, a ring stronghold, was "emancipated" by

Above: Nicholas Muller, the Tammany-allied boss of Richmond County, was the most powerful Democrat on Staten Island at his prime. *Courtesy of the Library of Congress.*

Left: Thomas C. Platt was a U.S. senator and the boss of the New York State Republican Party in the late nineteenth century and played an important role in the consolidation of the city. *Courtesy of the Library of Congress.*

the "complete turn-over in the local government" and the "complete throw-down of Mullerism."[741]

In late 1895 and early 1896, support for consolidation among Staten Islanders was tantamount to good government reform. This was likely further spurred by the fact that Platt turned to Senator Lexow, the champion of the anti-corruption committee, to carry the bill in the 1896 session. Richmond County's new crop of officials came out strongly in support of the measure, whether based on their own convictions or on the clear mandate provided by the citizenry. Doyle, now president of the board of supervisors, came out publicly in support of the consolidation plan,[742] as did the *Richmond County Advance*, whose sentiments changed as the idea that the new government could hold ring rule at bay took hold. The paper openly fantasized that "some of the kickers who have hampered and clogged the consolidation will be removed to another and a better world."[743]

With Lexow shepherding the legislation, it moved quickly, passing the legislature on April 22. Governor Morton signed it on May 11, after a few weeks of back and forth over who would control of the next steps, himself or Platt. It was to take effect on January 1, 1898, well in time for the 1900 census, and immediately form a charter commission to establish the city's new municipal government. As the most notable consolidationist and recognized "Father of Greater New York," Andrew Haswell Green topped the list of appointees. However, a bout with illness kept him from participating.[744]

For Staten Island, Morton recommended George Pinney,[745] the president of the Staten Island Good Government Club and the 1895 winner for Castleton supervisor.[746] He served as the commission's secretary. Though a Republican, he was regarded by the governor as independent from Platt and thus could be a check on any commission plan to replace Tammany with a machine under the "easy boss."[747] Needing a further bulwark, Morton appointed Seth Low, the twenty-third mayor of Brooklyn and a leading progressive reformer. He would serve as chairman of the committee on the draft, tasked with tying all of the various proposals together. However, the reform faction would be overshadowed, so much so that Low and others would later file a supplementary report condemning the entire process.[748]

As the charter commission got underway, it became evident that amassing Republican control in the new city was the clear goal of Platt. His allies, eager to placate the Brooklyn's delegation's desire to maintain some independence and to shore up GOP chances, favored a borough approach as opposed to subdividing power over smaller neighborhood-sized subdivisions. Additionally, each borough would be treated as a quasi-independent school

Seth Low, a leading
progressive reformer, served
as the twenty-third mayor
of Brooklyn and the ninety-
second mayor of New York.
*Courtesy of the Library of
Congress.*

district.[749] Writing just two years after the charter commission, historian Ira K. Morris noted that for Richmond County, the board of supervisors—the true powerbase of county government—would be abolished and replaced by a borough board, which would lose the ability to issue bonds for new debt but would have the power to draw up the local legislative subdivisions. In that way, the existing power structure would partially survive.[750]

Platt hoped that under this new system Republicans could retain power, in the event they were unable win the mayoralty, through borough presidents and their appointments in Brooklyn, Queens, the Bronx and Staten Island. In the end, the charter commission's final product was a document so convoluted, confusing and seemingly corrupt that even Tammany Democrats supported its adoption.[751] The charter bill had to be rushed through the state legislature in part so that the public wouldn't have time to digest what it entailed. As James W. Pryor, a contemporary political scientist, wrote, "The view that it was more important to have Greater New York as soon as possible, rather than bring the city into being under conditions as favorable as the time and deliberation could make them, has prevailed."[752] The commission's final draft was submitted to the legislature in late February and soon passed, only months before the charter governing 3 million people was to go into effect.[753]

ELECTIONS FOR A GREATER CITY

As the calendar moved toward consolidation day, the focus of the city's body politic shifted to the election of November 2, 1897, which would determine who governs the behemoth. Whoever won those contests would be sworn into office on January 1 and handed the reins of Greater New York, along with its thirty-five-thousand-person workforce and $100 million budget.

The new city's Good Government reformers saw this as an opportunity to wrest the municipal patronage mill out of the hands of Tammany, once and for all. Since 1896, they had been planning for this moment and had formed a third party, called the Citizens Union, which hoped to permanently emancipate Greater New York from the chains of machine politics. As their standard-bearer, they nominated Seth Low for mayor.[754]

Tammany went with a traditional pick, an obscure judge named Robert Van Wyck, who had little recognition and no access to money and lacked charisma. Boss Croker emerged to quarterback this race, undoubtedly picking Van Wyck on his one crucial characteristic: pliability.[755] As the *Tribune* summarized on the night of his nominating convention, "Several men of higher reputation, stronger character and greater popularity were considered, and the choice made can only be explained on the theory that the bosses thought Judge Van Wyck weak enough to be implicitly controlled."[756] For comptroller, the second-highest office in the new government, Croker similarly chose Bird Coler, a man whom the paper claimed "was probably never heard of by nine-tenths of the delegates before they were told to vote for him."[757]

On Staten Island, Muller did not have as simple a time getting his slate nominated through the county Democratic Party as his Manhattan counterpart. The anti-ring forces were as vocal as ever in the fall of 1897. Muller topped his county ticket with the name of Dr. John L. Feeny for president of the borough of Richmond; like the boss, he was a Tammany acolyte for as many years as he'd been involved in politics.[758] Muller hoped that a win would assist in Croker's plan to consolidate the boroughs' five Democratic machines into one big Tammany tiger, with an eye toward national dominance.[759] Feeny had served as Muller's delegate to a gathering

Robert Van Wyck was the Tammany nominee for mayor in the first election for office in Greater New York. *Courtesy of the New York Public Library.*

of Tammany Democratic allies in the weeks prior, where the plans were hatched for the upcoming campaign in a smoke-filled saloon on Broadway.[760] Not to mention, three years earlier, Feeny served on the board of supervisor's finance committee, where alongside two other ring stalwarts, he effectively gave control of the county's purse strings to the Muller machine.[761] For Staten Islanders, there could be no doubt that support for Feeny was support for Muller—and support for Muller was support for Tammany.

Erastus Wiman had hoped to stifle the Muller Ring's plans from the inside, through the fracture of Richmond's Democratic organization. He had been appearing at events for several weeks, denouncing the condition of workingmen and proposing that the new port of Greater New York be a "free port" to spur on manufacturing and prosperity.[762] He formed an alliance with the Democratic organization forming behind the candidacy of Henry George, a popular economist and former mayoral contender.[763] These and other reformers banded to support a second Democratic line on the November 2 ballot in the county. Muller was incensed and filed lawsuit to prevent the nominating petitions for the "Jeffersonian Democrats," a name they borrowed, from being accepted. The court ruled against them, and the county clerk was permitted to print ballots with candidates nominated by Wiman and the George faction under that banner, as well as separate lines for the United Dems and, of course, the Citizens Union. Wiman himself appeared on the ballot for City Council under the Jeffersonian and United Democrats.[764]

For borough president, opposition to the ring was unified. The Jeffersonian Dems, United Dems and the Citizen Union all backed the Republican nominee, George Cromwell, of Southfield.[765] The united front presented the greatest challenge to Muller in what was arguably the most important race for him and his cronies. Under the new charter, the borough president would preside over the borough board and have an *ex officio* seat on the city's most powerful deciding bodies. In essence, the office had the most authority in the county to divvy the patronage that fueled the machine; thus, preventing Mueller's control over it rose above traditional partisan politics.

If sticking the fork into the Tammany machine was the true goal of Platt, as it was for many Staten Islanders, surely he would see the benefit of also uniting a fusion ticket in the citywide races alongside the Citizens Union and the smaller Democratic Party lines as well. In fact, he was prepared to do so. However, Low's nomination came early in the process, and Republicans felt angered at having been outmaneuvered and placed on their back foot by the reformers. Many Republicans soon believed that they "would prefer to have [the city] under organization control, and they [were] shocked at the bad manners of the Citizens Union in putting Mr. Low so early in the field."[766] Ever the pragmatist, Platt approached Elihu Root, the leader of the Citizens Union but formerly a stalwart Republican on national matters, about cutting the Republican organization in on a percentage of the patronage jobs. Root balked.[767]

Less than a week after the Citizens Unions nominated Low, Lemuel Quigg, congressman and president of the New York Republican county committee, declared that "under no circumstances will the Republican organization accept Mr. Low for Mayor."[768] Platt added, "The forcing process never worked well on the Republican party, and it will be no more successful this year than heretofore."[769] They announced a straight Republican ticket, with Benjamin Tracy, former secretary of the navy, as their nominee for mayor.

The race between the three mayoral candidates was unpredictable. There were fault lines along traditional Republican and Democrat fractures, as well as those who favored reforming traditional machine rule. Additionally, it was hard to judge the turnout of what would actually be the first time the larger electorate of Greater New York voted as one unit. Almost as soon as the ballot was set, there was wild speculation. Lieutenant Governor Timothy Woodruff believed that Seth Low would serve as a spoiler for the GOP, throwing the election to Tammany.[770] Even faraway newspapers like the *Providence Journal* took notice of how weak the Democrats were that year.[771] Letters to the editor urged Republican voters to do their "duty" by voting for Low, "the one honest candidate in the field" and "puppet neither of Croker nor Platt."[772] The Citizens Union candidate certainly had gained momentum and was clearly pulling support from the Republican ticket. At a Brooklyn GOP rally that October, reporters noted the "hearty and prolonged applause for Seth Low" when Tracy, their own candidate, happened to mention his name.[773] At Low's own rally at Carnegie Hall, described as the "most solidly enthusiastic and altogether the most significant ratification meeting of the present campaign,"[774] prominent Republicans spoke boldly in his favor. Oddsmakers on Wall Street gave two-to-one odds that Low would win.[775]

By November, it had became clear that Platt feared a Low win far more than Van Wyck—machine rule being better than reform, after all, even if it wasn't his machine. He understood that Croker was a man who would always be willing to make a deal, and so he did not bother hiding the fact that the Republican machine would prefer Tammany running the new city hall.[776] News headlines screamed, "The Machines in Accord—Every Effort Will Be Made to Defeat Low."[777] Quigg confirmed to inquisitive reporters that they were in battle against Low and not Van Wyck, and Tammany's candidate for district attorney chimed in, "Of the Republicans, I have nothing to say. Our fight is with Low."[778]

In Richmond County, unlike Manhattan and Brooklyn, there was little daylight between the Republican and Citizens Union organizations. Cromwell was running under both banners and was the only citywide or borough-wide candidate on the ballot in the five boroughs to be cross-endorsed by each party.[779] Furthermore, Richmond's delegates to the Republican City Convention, along with those of Queens, were part of the 49 out of 348 who voted against Platt to give Seth Low the party's nomination over Tracy.[780] The easy boss's response was an unsuccessful attempt to eradicate the county committees and place all the power in a larger city committee under his control.[781]

On October 28, Low completed a campaign swing through the five boroughs with a visit to Staten Island, where he spoke at a German club in Stapleton and an auditorium near Prohibition Park. Each audience gave him a "hearty welcome" that was "cordial in the extreme."[782] At 9:30 p.m., the candidate rolled up to Prohibition Park in an elaborately illuminated and decorated trolley car. He entered the packed University Temple, a four-thousand-seat hall near Boulevard and Willard Avenues,[783] just as another speaker was delivering his remarks. But as soon the crowd caught sight of Low walking onto the sawdust-covered floor of the main room, they loudly demanded "three cheers for Seth Low," to the chagrin of a small Tracy clique that had been heckling from the upper galleries.[784] The crowds were decidedly anti-Tammany. George Cromwell, who spoke just ahead of Low, tried to shore up his support among reform-minded Citizen Union voters with potshots at machine rule, delivering an "effective and well received little speech."[785] The real enthusiasm was saved for the mayoral candidate, who received a full two-minute applause upon taking the stage, as a contingent of young girls from the Mariners Harbor School joined him in waving banners and American flags. He addressed the crowd and vowed better public schools, stressed the need to maintain local control and cited the shameful record of Tammany Hall. He warned the audience that "no part of Greater New York will be more affected by consolidation than Staten Island" and urged them to vote for the Citizens Union ticket, including Cromwell, which is "made up of men pledged solely to work for the city and not to build up any organization."[786] At the German Club, he again highlighted his commitment to those on his ticket and asked the audience to elect "so fine a man as George Cromwell" to thunderous applause.[787]

DESPITE THE ENTHUSIASM SURROUNDING Seth Low going into the election, the day would not be won by the Citizens Union. In what the *Times* called a "complete victory," the initial results from the election on Tuesday, November 2, showed a Tammany win for every city and borough-wide office.[788] The *Tribune* declared, "Tammany Sweeps the City"[789] and called it "The Triumph of the Tiger," while lamenting that the machine would have now control of $75 million in patronage.[790] Croker, who took the returns in a spacious parlor at the Murray Hill Hotel, smugly chastised the "fake journalism" that had been critical of Tammany and opined that this proved New Yorkers "are tired of reformers of amateur stripe."[791]

In total, Van Wyck's plurality was more than eighty thousand votes more than Low, who finished second, with Tracy in a distant third. In Richmond, Muller's machine was able to scrape together a decent two-thousand-vote margin for Van Wyck over Tracy, the second-place finisher.[792] Tammany's astounding win ensured that despite any and all hope of eliminating machine rule in the new city, the bosses would run the show. By the time Van Wyck sat behind his desk for the first time on January 1, 1898, the patronage game had played out. "Slowly but surely the big wheel of the mill which is grinding out the patronage in the various municipal departments to the Tammany braves went 'round and 'round yesterday," wrote the *Times*, "and at every turn a new member of the 'army of expectancy' was made happy."[793] The attempt to consolidate the cities, counties and towns around the harbor into Greater New York as a means to eradicate corruption was an abject failure.

A LIGHT IN THE DARKNESS

On November 4, when the results were published, Feeny received 5,423 votes, accruing 77 more than his Republican opponent and out-polling his fellow Democrat, Robert Van Wyck, by more than 550 votes. Citing irregularities, Republicans balked and immediately demanded a recount.

On November 18, after an exhaustive effort, the Richmond County Board of Canvassers—the arbiters of elections at that time—ruled that George Cromwell had actually received 5,427 votes, thus squeaking ahead of Feeny by a razor-sharp margin. (It also found 1 additional vote for Feeny too.) The board declared the Republican the victor, but Tammany lawyers took the matter to court.[794]

The Democratic Party's lawsuit brought the matter before Richmond County Supreme Court justice J.O. Dykman, who ordered another recount. At issue were about 200 votes from the town of Middletown, where allegations of fraudulent activities were rampant. At the end of the proceedings and tallies, the new count stood at 5,446 for Feeny and 5,405 for Cromwell. The judge ordered the county canvassers to certify the new results, making Feeny the winner. Fifty-one years before "Dewey defeats Truman," the *Times* ran the headline, "Dr. Feeny Gets the Office."[795]

Cromwell vowed to fight, but Feeny was sworn in on the spot on December 16 to the cheers of an awaiting crowd outside the courthouse, although he could not officially take office until January 1.[796] Within two weeks, Republican lawyers had brought an appeal of Dykman's decision to the appellate court in Brooklyn. On the first day of the proceeding, the court began reinstating some of the Cromwell votes thrown out by the original ruling. Justice Cullen, one of the five on the panel, motioned that ballots made by an "unlawful act," by which he described the mere marking of the ballot in an imprecise location, should not disenfranchise that voter. Just 103 years before America fought over "hanging chads," Staten Islanders battled over Cromwell voters who had simply marked their ballots in the square containing his name but not the circle adjacent to the name delineating the proper spot.[797] On December 29, just three days before the consolidation would go into effect, the Appellate Division ruled unanimously on the final adjudication of 184 ballots. On one, the 185th, the vote was four to one. The outcome was made more remarkable by the fact that Democrats had a three-to-two majority on the court over Republicans.[798] The presiding judge declared George Cromwell the de facto winner; however, the court required yet another recount whereby ballots would be counted under the new criteria.[799]

Soon it was the Feeny camp vowing to fight on by taking the case to the Court of Appeals, the highest in New York, hoping for a declaration that the appellate judges had created too broad of a criterion for counting votes.[800] This would take time, and a last-minute attempt in Richmond County Supreme Court on December 31 by Republicans to get an order for Cromwell to be sworn in failed. The judge would leave the decision to the court of last resort.[801]

That night, as rain dampened the mood, Brooklyn's Mayor Frederick Wurster and six of its former mayors gathered in the Common Council chamber of Brooklyn City Hall, within hours to be renamed Borough Hall, to observe the sun setting of America's third-largest city. "Calmly and with dignity," observed the *Brooklyn Daily Eagle*, "Brooklyn passed from her state as an independent city into the Greater New York."[802] The evening wore on, and county elders, using their orations to encourage a fight to preserve its identity, marked the ceremony with speeches. It concluded with a reading of a somber poem entitled "The Passing of Brooklyn." As the clock struck midnight, the great bell on the building's roof tolled, marking for all in earshot the birth of the new borough.[803]

At noon the following day, across the river, a less elaborate ceremony marked the transfer of power to Mayor Van Wyck. A small band played as he greeted throngs of well-wishers who had packed the halls of city hall.[804] Surely, Nick Muller and the leaders of the Richmond County ring were among them, as the underlying purpose for most attendees was to ensure their seat on the patronage train. One famous Tammany district leader, George Washington Plunkitt, bluntly told the new mayor that the machine loyalists from his district were on hand en masse, "and every man wants a job."[805] Plunkitt would go on to have a fulfilling career in Tammany politics and would even coin the term "honest graft" just a few years later.[806] At 12:55 p.m., with pleasantries limited to an hour, Van Wyck retired back into his smoky office with Croker's right-hand man, John Carroll, to begin filling the new city's payroll with Tammany braves.[807]

On the eve of consolidation, Staten Island hadn't played host to any formal events. That afternoon, the various county boards met for the final time, with little work to be done and few words to mark the conclusion of their business. Knowing that their debts would soon be guaranteed by the new city, the Edgewater Board of Trustees approved a $15,000 contract for 150 new streetlights, while the Southfield Town Board awarded $75,000 for contract to macadamize roads and a whopping $100,000 for the construction of the one-hundred-foot-wide boulevard that would eventually become the longest road in the new city and bear the name of a future mayor, John Hylan.[808] Dr. Feeny, acting in his role as president of the board of supervisors, pledged to continue the work of governing the county until a transition was complete. The gossip columns of New York newspapers took notice of the Island's grandest social event that evening, which took place at the Dongan Hill's clubhouse of the Richmond County Hunt Club, also known as the Richmond County Country Club. The ballroom was "banked with palms and potted plants, and the walls and ceilings were festooned with similax, holly and bunting."[809] The dancing began at 10:30 p.m., and among the crowd were the county's elite, like the Outerbridge family, who were charter members of the club, and Mr. and Mrs. Charles Pfizer, the notable German-born pharmaceutical chemist. At midnight, the crowd sung the obligatory "Auld Lang Syne," followed by a series of the club's favorite hunting songs.[810] No one, at least publicly, mourned the loss of Richmond's self-determination or toasted to the prosperity of Greater New York.

The next day, there was no ceremony marking the transfer of power. In fact, there was no transfer of power at all, as the county court did not lift the stay preventing Cromwell's ascension on the day he was set to be sworn in as one of the five borough presidents. On day one, Richmond had no executive and no representative on the numerous boards on which the borough president held an *ex officio* seat or an appointee. Many more such days would follow.[811]

The Court of Appeals' decision was expected any day, but January turned into February and still Richmond lacked a borough president. Finally in May, the tribunal upheld the decision of the Appellate Division and once again demanded that the board of canvassers meet again to recount the ballots. In this instance, it found Mr. Cromwell to have won by a margin of twenty votes and moved to recertify the results. For Feeny, the fight still didn't end.[812]

On June 1, Cromwell stepped into a portrait-laden room at city hall that served as the meeting place for the board of public improvements, an important body under the original city charter that had jurisdiction to spend immeasurable sums of money on public contracts. Citing Feeny's renewed appeals to the Richmond County Supreme Court, the board, led by Mayor Van Wyck, declined to honor his credentials and refused to seat him.[813] The Tammany tigers were not going to let an outsider sit on this public body if there was any hope against it. Three weeks later, Cromwell again tried to take his seat. This time, the borough president of Queens, a machine man himself, made a motion that his Staten Island counterpart be seated. It was again rejected by the board on the grounds that it needed to await the opinion of the city's newly appointed corporation counsel.[814]

Finally, on the last day of June 1898, Borough President Cromwell was allowed his seat on the board of public improvements.[815] Justice Daly of the Richmond County Supreme Court issued a writ mandating that the new police board, which concurrently served as the city's board of canvassers under the new charter, meet to certify the election results reached by the county's board back in May. Cromwell was the winner by twenty votes, once and for all.[816]

Back on Staten Island, on August 29, 1898, Borough President George Cromwell convened his borough board for the first time to take up a long list of public projects and appointments that sat queued for approval.[817] It was the only governing body of New York City not to be controlled by Tammany Hall.

Epilogue

The corrupt machine held a solid grip on the first mayoralty of Greater New York. Its acolytes filled the public service rolls, and its allies reaped the benefits of lucrative city contracts. Years later, when Van Wyck passed away in his Paris home, his obituary in the *Times* unflatteringly read, "As Mayor, Mr. Van Wyck became involved in probably more administrative scandals than any Mayor in the city's history. He stood as the representative of Tammany Hall, the personal selection of Richard Croker, then in full power as the boss of the organization."[818]

Van Wyck survived an attempt at removal by the young governor Theodore Roosevelt but was defeated in 1901 in reelection by Seth Low, who managed to finally form a fusion ticket of the Citizens Union and Republican Parties. On Staten Island, the ticket helped George Cromwell score two more full terms, serving through 1913.

In each borough, there was a rush to capitalize on the infrastructure that was promised to accompany consolidation. Yet within its first year, Greater New York's combined bond and contract debt already exceeded state constitutional limits. Even Tammany's handpicked comptroller was forced to admit that "extravagant contracts, intended to bind the city for five, ten and even twenty years, were entered upon with no apparent purpose other than to benefit favored local or individual interests."[819] Other public works, regardless of importance, simply had to wait.

When the county's contract with B&O Railroad for Staten Island Ferry Service was to expire, there was a fight to get the new government to

Staten Island Borough Hall has been the seat of the borough's limited government since its completion in 1906. *Courtesy of the New York Public Library.*

assume its operation, even as the city went through on plans for connections between the four other boroughs. Richmond's residents marched on city hall in February 1903, demanding Mayor Low reject the proposal to continue with a costly privately operated contract. David Tysen's memoir records the meeting of city's Sinking Funds Commission, in which he and others demanded a municipal ferry and expressed their indignation at being forced to pay "for putting our feet on the soil of Manhattan," a burden the residents of other boroughs need not shoulder. "[W]hen we consider the vast amount the City has spent in bridges and tunnels to connect the other boroughs," he said, "and they get the benefits for all these great improvements and we didn't, it would be a burlesque upon justice to deny to Richmond the cost of a good ferry."[820]

The municipal takeover of the Staten Island Ferry did, of course, occur under Borough President Cromwell, but the fight for much of Richmond County's needs with respect to the greater city have been framed in the same terms ever since. Tysen and Cromwell went on to fight for equitable transfers for ferry passengers to the transit system shortly thereafter, using essentially the same argument.[821]

For decades, Richmond Borough desired a hard connection with the rest of the city, all while connections between its four sisters proceeded on pace. Geography was an issue, for certain, but reasonable proposals to connect the Island with the public transit system of its own city went nowhere. The Staten Island Chamber of Commerce and Civic League proposed a rail tunnel connection to the southern tip of Manhattan through New Jersey. It would have originated in Tompkinsville, traveling under the Kill and along the Jersey coastline and Ellis Island before crossing the Hudson River at the Battery. Since it would have required legislation and cooperation from both states, the city never pursued it.[822]

One plan did initially get off the ground: a tunnel connecting the Staten Island Rapid Transit with Brooklyn's Fourth Avenue rail line (now the R). Mayor Hylan supported the project after planners and rail companies agreed to make it wide enough to "take an elephant,"[823] meaning freight would also be hauled side by side with commuters to regional connections in New Jersey. The borough's 120,000 residents, despite buttering up the mayor by naming their longest thoroughfare after him, were deemed unworthy of a standalone passenger line. Nonetheless, in 1923, Hylan posed with pickaxe in hand alongside Borough President John Lynch and former borough president Calvin Van Name to break ground on the new tunnel.[824] The plan was abandoned just two years later, after new projections estimated that the cost would exceed $60 million, 200 percent higher than originally estimated. Four hundred years after Verrazzano sailed through the Narrows, city planners began dreaming up an alternative option: a bridge.[825]

It would be thirty years before the Port Authority and Triborough Bridge and Tunnel Authority, under its chairman, Robert Moses, even began the studies necessary to undertake construction of the then longest suspension bridge in the world. In 1964, Staten Islanders were finally physically connected with the four other boroughs of which they had been joined politically for sixty-six years. By then, connections between Manhattan and Brooklyn, Queens and the Bronx had all long been completed. Nine crossed the East River alone.

The Verrazzano-Narrows Bridge was to connect to a vast system of highways on Staten Island to accommodate the growing needs of the borough's driving public. After all, with no rail connection to the rest of the city, could anyone expect its residents to commute any other way? Only half of Robert Moses's planned routes got built, but the lack of the Wolfe's Pond Parkway, the Shorefront Drive and completed Willowbrook (now Martin Luther King Jr. Expressway) and Richmond (now Korean War Veterans) Parkways would have undoubtedly eased traffic woes. There is, after all, still no rail link.

When it came to placing undesirable facilities around New York City, however, planners had no problem finding Richmond County on the map. Robert Moses and other officials supported the opening of a temporary landfill for municipal waste at Fresh Kills in 1947, before making it permanent and turning it into the largest in the world in 1955. It led to the first calls for the secession of Staten Island from the city by one of the county's two assemblymen, Edmund Radigan.[826] It went nowhere, but Fresh Kills would become a rallying cry in the early 1990s attempt at secession, in which a full two-thirds of the county voted in favor of a schism.[827]

Fresh Kills may be the most iconic example of a moment when the city's broader political class made a decision that was detrimental to Staten Island and over the objection of local elected representatives. It certainly would not be the only one.

In 1963, the city designated Annadale and Huguenot, then just a collection of one-lane wooded roads, as an urban renewal area. For Mayor John Lindsay, that didn't go far enough, and in 1966, he ordered a moratorium on all sales of city-owned lots in the 15,600 acres that made up the south shore. His South Richmond Plan would have developed it with blocks of utopian apartment buildings for roughly 450,000 people. Thankfully, it, too, was stopped by local politicians, bolstered by support from the recently formed New York State Conservative Party.[828] Staten Island's population would be more than double its current number had the plan came to fruition.

Over the years, proposals that would have hurt Staten Island have come and gone, and it has continuously fallen on local elected officials to point out just how poorly we are served by a city government in which we have little say. Guy Molinari, the outspoken congressman and borough president, successfully opposed four homeless shelters, only to watch Mayor Koch alter his plan to use vacant land for an equally unpopular new city jail in Rossville. This as Richmond's percentage of both the city's homeless and its incarcerated population were fractional.[829] Homeless shelter fights would occur somewhat often in the borough, as the Bill de Blasio administration can attest. His predecessor was not much better for the borough—the Bloomberg administration hiked property taxes and sought to build a waste-to-energy trash incineration plant in Travis.

There can be no doubt that being a part of New York City has had its benefits for Staten Island, and if nothing else, the borough has surely gained from city employment, with thousands of its residents part of the municipal workforce.

Yet, perhaps it is time to ask the question again: What price has been paid for the privilege of being part of New York City? Certainly, there were those in the late nineteenth century who contemplated what was to be lost with consolidation, and it would be unfair to simply suppose they were wrong. For many, the Island was worth preserving as it was, and perhaps it still is.

Notes

Chapter 1

1. Richard M. Bayles, ed., *History of Richmond County (Staten Island) New York, From Its Discovery to the Present Time* (New York: I.E. Preston & Company, 1887), 253.
2. J.J. Clute, *Annals of Staten Island, From Its Discovery to the Present Time* (New York: Press of Chas. Vogt, 1877), 70.
3. Charles W. Leng and William T. Davis, *Staten Island and Its People: A History, 1629–1929*, vol. 1 (New York: Lewis Historical, 1930–33), 202.
4. *The Revised Statutes of the State of New York, as Altered by the Legislature; Including the Statutory Provisions of a General Nature, Passed from 1828 to 1835 Inclusive; With References to Judicial Decisions; to Which Are Added, Certain Local Acts Passed Before and Since the Revised Statutes; All the Acts of General Interest Passed During the Session of 1836; and an Appendix, Containing Extracts from the Original Reports of the Revisers to the Legislature, All Material Notes Which Accompanied Those Reports, and Explanatory Remarks*, "List of Towns," vol. 3 (Albany, NY: Packard and Van Benthuysen, 1836), 308.
5. Henry G. Steinmeyer, *Staten Island: 1525–1898* (Staten Island, NY: Staten Island Historical Society, 1987), 42.
6. Town records of Westfield, quoted in Leng and Davis, *Staten Island and Its People*, 1:205.
7. Ibid.
8. Clute, *Annals of Staten Island*, 142–45.

9. Leng and Davis, *Staten Island and Its People*, 1:206.

10. Clute, *Annals of Staten Island*, 445–46.

11. Leng and Davis, *Staten Island and Its People*, 1:502 and 206.

12. Bayles, *History of Richmond County*, 251.

13. Leng and Davis, *Staten Island and Its People*, 1:207.

14. Numerous records exist for the appointment of surveyors and the plans to lay roads, in John Stillwell, ed., *Historical and Genealogical Miscellany: Data Relating to the Settlement and Settlers of New York and New Jersey*, vol. 1. (New York, 1903), 35–56; Leng and Davis, *Staten Island and Its People*, 1:137.

15. Leng and Davis, *Staten Island and Its People*, 1:222.

16. Ibid., 227, 296 and 343.

17. Donald R. Hickey, "Federalist Defense Policy in the Age of Jefferson, 1801–1812," *Military Affairs* 45, no. 2 (April 1981): 63–70, 64.

18. Clute, *Annals of Staten Island*, 149–50.

19. "News," *Republican Watch-Tower* (New York, NY), May 9, 1801.

20. "News," *The Columbian* (New York, NY), April 30, 1810.

21. "John McClean, Commissary of Military Stores Sworn," *American Citizen* (New York, NY), July 25, 1806.

22. Edwin G. Burrows and Mike Wallace, *Gotham: A History of New York City to 1898* (New York: Oxford University Press, 1999), 409.

23. Ibid.

24. "Funeral Procession of John Pearce," *New-York Commercial Advertiser* (New York, NY), April 26, 1806.

25. Burrows and Wallace, *Gotham*, 411.

26. Clute, *Annals of Staten Island*, 149.

27. "Mr. Cheetham," *Republican Watch-Tower* (New York, NY), September 15, 1807.

28. Burrows and Wallace, *Gotham*, 411.

29. "Celebration of the Thirty First Anniversary of American Independence, at Richmond, Staten Island, Saturday, July 4th, 1807," *Republican Watch-Tower* (New York, NY), July 10, 1807.

30. "New York," *Morning Chronicle* (New York, NY), April 3, 1806.

31. Andrew F. Fagal, "Terror Weapons in the Naval War of 1812," *New York History* 94, no. 3–4 (Summer/Fall 2013): 221–40.

32. Richard Beamish, *Memoir of the Life of Sir Marc Isambard Brunel* (London: Longman & Company, 1862), available at https://archive.org/stream/memoiroflifeofsi00beamuoft/memoiroflifeofsi00beamuoft_djvu.txt.

33. "Wednesday; Commissioner; Gentlemen; Richmond; Beach; Staten Island," *Public Advertiser* (New York, NY), December 31, 1808.

34. U.S. Department of Interior, National Park Service, *A History of Fort Wadsworth, New York Harbor*, Cultural Resource Management Study No. 7, ed. Frederick R. Black (Boston, MA, 1983), http://npshistory.com/publications/gate/fort-wadsworth-hrs.pdf.

35. Rene Chartrand, *Forts of the War of 1812* (Oxford, UK: Osprey Publishing, 2012), 18.

36. Steinmeyer, *Staten Island*, 43.

37. U.S. Department of Interior, National Parks Service, *History of Fort Wadsworth*.

38. "Blockade of Our Harbour," *Evening Post* (New York, NY), January 19, 1813.

39. Leng and Davis, *Staten Island and Its People*, 1:219.

40. U.S. Department of Interior, National Parks Service, *History of Fort Wadsworth*.

41. Charles M. Dow, "Daniel D. Tompkins," *Quarterly Journal of the New York State Historical Association* 1, no. 2 (January 1920): 7–13, 10.

42. Leng and Davis, *Staten Island and Its People*, 1:220.

43. U.S. Department of Interior, National Parks Service, *History of Fort Wadsworth*.

44. Dow, "Daniel D. Tompkins," 10.

45. Daniel D. Tompkins, "On the Indians and Slavery," *A Columbia College Student in the Eighteenth Century: Essays by Daniel D. Tompkins; Class of 1795; Sometime Governor of New York State and Vice President of the United States*, eds. Ray W. Irwin and Edna L. Jacobsen (New York: Columbia University Press, 1940), 4.

46. Daniel D. Tompkins to the State Legislature, January 28, 1817, New York State, *Messages from the Governors: Comprising Executive Communications to the Legislature and Other Papers Relating to Legislation from the Organization of the First Colonial Assembly in 1683 to and Including the Year 1906*, vol. 2, ed. Charles Z. Lincoln (Albany, NY: J.B. Lyon Company, 1909), 880.

47. Dow, "Daniel D. Tompkins," 12.

48. Leng and Davis, *Staten Island and Its People*, 1:221.

49. Clute, *Annals of Staten Island*, 318.

50. Leng and Davis, *Staten Island and Its People*, 1:222.

51. Clute, *Annals of Staten Island*, 318.

52. Brighton Heights Reformed Church, "Our Church History," http://www.bhrcforgod.org/writtenhistory.

53. Leng and Davis, *Staten Island and Its People*, 1:223.

54. Bayles, *History of Richmond County*, 484.

55. Ira K. Morris, *Morris's Memorial History of Staten Island, New York*, vol. 1 (New York: Memorial Publishing, 1898), 158.
56. Death Notice, *Evening Post* (New York, NY), September 15, 1836. Morris incorrectly lists the date as the fourteenth.
57. "Death of Aaron Burr," *Commercial Advertiser* (New York, NY), September 23, 1836.
58. Morris, *Morris's Memorial History of Staten Island*, 2:158.
59. Leng and Davis, *Staten Island and Its People*, 1:255.
60. Morris, *Morris's Memorial History of Staten Island*, 2:190.
61. F.L. Patton, ed., "Professor Joseph Kargé Ph.D.," *Princeton College Bulletin*, vols. 5–7 (Princeton, NJ: Princeton Press, 1896), 28.
62. Ibid., 26.
63. Leng and Davis, *Staten Island and Its People*, 1:256.
64. Ibid.
65. Susannah Cahalan, "Mex General's Staten Ex-Isle," *New York Post*, November 13, 2011.
66. H. Bailey Carroll, "Texas Collection," *Southwestern Historical Quarterly* 59, no. 4 (April 1956): 502–16, 502.
67. NPR, "'Chicle': A Chewy Story of the Americas," *NPR Special Series: The Week's Best Stories from NPR Books*, July 12, 2009, https://www.npr.org/templates/story/story.php?storyId=106439600.
68. "Thomas Adams Dead," *New York Times*, February 8, 1905.
69. H. Nelson Gay, "Garibaldi's American Contacts and His Claims to American Citizenship," *American Historical Review* 38, no. 1 (October 1932): 1–19, 7.
70. Howard Marraro, "Garibaldi in New York," *New York History* 27, no. 2 (April 1946): 179–203, 182.
71. Gay, "Garibaldi's American Contacts," 7–8.
72. Marraro, "Garibaldi in New York," 192–93.
73. Ibid., 200.
74. Garibaldi-Meucci Museum, "History of the House," http://pub1.andyswebtools.com/cgi-bin/p/awtp-custom.cgi?d=garibaldi-meucci-museum&page=749.
75. Barnett Shepherd, *Staten Island Scenery: Paintings, Prints, Drawings, and Photographs: 1679–1900* (Staten Island, NY: Staten Island Historical Society and Staten Island Museum, 2013), 75–76; Morris, *Morris's Memorial History of Staten Island*, 2:73.
76. New York Public Library, NYPL Map Warper: Map 17075, *Map of Staten Island, Richmond County, New York City, State of New York*.

77. Jasper Francis Cropsey to Marie Cropsey, July 7, 1850, reprinted in "'The Brushes He Painted with That Last Day Are There…': Jasper F. Cropsey's Letter to His Wife, Describing Thomas Cole's Home and Studio, July 1850," *American Art Journal* 16, no. 3 (Summer 1984): 78–83, 78.

78. Newington-Cropsey Foundation, "Biography," www.newingtoncropsey.com, http://www.newingtoncropsey.com/documents/JFC%20Biography%20web.pdf, Fig. 2. *Cropsey Farm, Staten Island*, 1843, oil on canvas (NCF 517; cat. No. 3).

79. Shepherd, *Staten Island Scenery*, 76.

80. Ibid.

81. Margaret Lundrigan, *Staten Island: Isle of the Bay* (Charleston, SC: Arcadia Publishing, 2004), 101.

82. New York Public Library, NYPL Map Warper: Layer 869, *Atlas of Staten Island, Richmond County, New York, from Official Records and Surveys; Compiled and Drawn by F.W. Beers.*

83. Morris, *Morris's Memorial History of Staten Island*, 2:74. Cropsey is actually buried in Sleepy Hollow, New York.

84. Newington-Cropsey Foundation, "Biography."

85. Ibid.

86. Kenneth W. Maddox, *The Unprejudiced Eye: The Drawings of Jasper F. Cropsey* (Yonkers, NY: Hudson River Museum, 1979), 61–62.

87. Barnett Shepherd, "Staten Island SEEN: 1679–1895," *Staten Island SEEN* (Staten Island, NY: Staten Island Museum, 2016), 32.

88. Milton Meltzer, *Henry David Thoreau: A Biography* (Minneapolis, MN: Twenty-First Century Books, 2007), 30.

89. Ibid.

90. Henry D. Thoreau to Sophie Thoreau, May 22, 1843, in Henry D. Thoreau, *The Correspondence of Henry David Thoreau*, eds. Walter Harding and Carl Bode (New York: New York University Press, 1958), 105.

91. Clyde L. MacKenzie Jr., *The Fisheries of Raritan Bay* (New Brunswick, NJ: Rutgers University Press, 1992), 27–28.

92. Barnett Shepherd, *Tottenville: The Town the Oyster Built* (Staten Island, NY: Tottenville Historical Society, 2010), 38.

93. "An Act for the Preservation of Oysters At & Near Richmond County in This Colony," passed December 16, 1737, in *The Colonial Laws of New York from the Year 1664 to the Revolution*, vol. 2, 1,067–68.

94. Shepherd, *Tottenville*, 38.

95. Bayles, *History of Richmond County*, 710.

NOTES TO PAGES 28–31

96. Shepherd, *Tottenville*, 39–52. The map referred to is *Butler's Map*, 1853, detail, James Butler, *Map of Staten Island or Richmond County, New York*, New York, Mayer and Company, copy in the collection of the Staten Island Museum.
97. Leng and Davis, *Staten Island and Its People*, 1:225–26.
98. Ibid., 226.
99. "Staten Island Manufactures," *Richmond County Mirror* 1, no. 1 (July 7, 1837), New Brighton, NY.
100. Leng and Davis, *Staten Island and Its People*, 1:226.
101. "Sienite Granite of Staten Island, for Sale," *Commercial Advertiser* (New York, NY), January 14, 1840.
102. "Cards of Business," *New York & Richmond County Free Press* (New York, NY), July 27, 1833.
103. Leng and Davis, *Staten Island and Its People*, 1:230. Leng cites the New York Agricultural Society report of 1842.
104. Ibid.
105. Leng and Davis, *Staten Island and Its People*, 1:231.
106. Ibid., 226.
107. "Public Sales," *Commercial Advertiser* (New York, NY), June 25, 1841.
108. Weymer J. Mills, "Romances of Summer Resorts," *The Delineator* 68, no. 1 (September 1905), New York: Butterick Publishing Company, 1905), 404.
109. Leng and Davis, *Staten Island and Its People*, 1:227.
110. Ibid.
111. New York Public Library, NYPL Map Warper: Map 17065, *Map of Staten Island, Richmond County. 16 Views of Buildings on Border. Also View of Elliottville the Property of Dr. S.M. Elliott*, http://maps.nypl.org/warper/maps/17065.
112. Ibid., Map 17063, *Map of Staten Island o Richmond County: 16 Views of Buildings on Border. Also View of Elliottville the Property of Dr. S.M. Elliott*, http://maps.nypl.org/warper/maps/17063.
113. Ibid., Map 17065.
114. Ibid., Map 17064, *Map of Staten Island o Richmond County: 16 Views of Buildings on Border. Also View of Elliottville the Property of Dr. S.M. Elliott*, http://maps.nypl.org/warper/maps/17064.
115. Ibid., Map 17060, *Map of Staten Island o Richmond County: 16 Views of Buildings on Border. Also View of Elliottville the Property of Dr. S.M. Elliott*, http://maps.nypl.org/warper/maps/17060.
116. Leng and Davis, *Staten Island and Its People*, 1:230.

117. William A. Croffut, *The Vanderbilts and the Story of Their Fortune* (New York: Bedford, Clarke & Company, 1886), 6–7.

118. Ibid.; New York Public Library, NYPL Map Warper: Layer 869.

119. "Commodore Vanderbilt: Where He Was Born—an Error Corrected—More Data," *Richmond County Advance* (West New Brighton, NY), January 11, 1902.

120. Croffut, *The Vanderbilts*, 7–22.

121. Bayles, *History of Richmond County*, 687.

122. Ibid.

123. "City Intelligence," *Commercial Advertiser* (New York, NY), June 1, 1860.

124. Leng and Davis, *Staten Island and Its People*, 1:239.

125. Clute, *Annals of Staten Island*, 440–41.

126. "The Political Mirror: Public Meeting at Factoryville," *Richmond County Mirror*, January 20, 1838.

127. Ibid.; Franklin B. Hough, ed., *The New York Civil List, Containing the Names and Origin of the Civil Divisions, and the Names and Dates of Election of Appointment of the Principal State and County Officers, from the Revolution to the Present Time* (Albany, NY: Weed, Parsons & Company, 1861), 362.

128. Leng and Davis, *Staten Island and Its People*, 1:239.

129. Clute, *Annals of Staten Island*, 440.

130. Andrew Robertson, "'Look on This Picture…and On This!': Nationalism, Localism and Partisan Images of Otherness in the United States, 1787–1820," *American Historical Review* 106, no. 4 (October 2001): 1,263–80, 1,271.

131. Joseph Hardwick, "The Church of England and English Clergymen in the United States, 1783–1861," in *English Ethnicity and Culture in North America*, ed. David T. Gleeson (Columbia: University of South Carolina Press, 2017), 4, ebook edition.

132. Leng and Davis, *Staten Island and Its People*, 1:216.

133. Ibid.

134. Bayles, *History of Richmond County*, 253.

135. Leng and Davis, *Staten Island and Its People*, 1:237.

136. Ibid., 241.

137. Ibid., 252.

138. Ibid.; New York Public Library, NYPL Map Warper: Layer 869.

139. Leng and Davis, *Staten Island and Its People*, 1:268.

140. "Local News," *Richmond County Gazette*, March 7, 1860.

141. "New York State: Estimate of Election Results," *New York Times*, November 5, 1860.

142. "The New Town—Rapid Progress!" *Richmond County Gazette*, April 4, 1860.

143. Clute, *Annals of Staten Island*, 148; Leng and Davis, *Staten Island and Its People*, 1:277.

144. Michael Birkner, "The New York–New Jersey Boundary Controversy, John Marshall and the Nullification Crisis," *Journal of the Early Republic* 12, no. 2 (Summer 1992): 195–212, 199.

145. Hon. James Parker, "A Brief History of the Boundary Disputes between New York and New Jersey," *Proceedings of the New Jersey Historical Society*, vol. 6, 1851–53 (Newark, NJ: printed at the Daily Advertiser Office, 1853), 107.

146. Ibid., 108.

147. Birkner, "New York–New Jersey Boundary Controversy," 205.

148. Parker, "Brief History of the Boundary Disputes," 108.

149. Leng and Davis, *Staten Island and Its People*, 1:262–63.

150. The Executive Committee of Staten Island, *Facts and Documents Bearing upon the Legal and Moral Questions Connected with the Recent Destruction of the Quarantine Buildings on Staten Island* (New York: WM C. Bryant & Company, 1858), 5.

151. Leng and Davis, *Staten Island and Its People*, 1:249–51.

152. Henry David Thoreau to Helen Thoreau, July 21, 1843, as quoted in Leng and Davis, *Staten Island and Its People*, 1:246.

153. Executive Committee of Staten Island, *Facts and Documents*, 14.

154. William Gribbin, "Divine Providence of Miasma? The Yellow Fever Epidemic of 1822," *New York History* 53, no. 3 (July 1972): 282–98, 282.

155. Leng and Davis, *Staten Island and Its People*, 1:263–64.

156. Executive Committee of Staten Island, *Facts and Documents*, 7.

157. Ibid., 6.

158. Ibid.

159. Ibid.

160. Ibid.

161. "Seguine's Point Matters Nature of the Hospital and Other Accommodation Being Furnished," *New York Herald*, July 3, 1857.

162. "Attack on the Police at Seguine's Point," *New York Daily Tribune*, July 13, 1857.

163. Ibid.

164. "The Excitement at Quarantine the Building Threatened to Be Demolished the Police on Duty All Night," *New York Herald*, March 7, 1858.

165. "Commissioners of Health," *Commercial Advertiser*, August 30, 1858.

166. Executive Committee of Staten Island, *Facts and Documents*, 10.
167. Leng and Davis, *Staten Island and Its People*, 1:265.
168. "Incendiarism on Staten Island: Burning of the Quarantine Buildings, and the Health Officer's Residence," *Commercial Advertiser*, September 2, 1858.
169. "More Arson at Staten Island," *Evening Post* (New York, NY), September 3, 1858.
170. "The Quarantine War: One Hundred Policemen on the Ground—The Sick in Tents—Order Restored," *Evening Post*, September, 4, 1858.
171. Leng and Davis, *Staten Island and Its People*, 1:267.

Chapter 2

172. Joseph C.G. Kennedy, *Population of the United States in 1860; Compiled from the Original Returns of The Eighth Census, Under the Direction of the Secretary of the Interior* (Washington, D.C.: Government Printing Office, 1864), 322–25.
173. Ibid., 325.
174. Burrows and Wallace, *Gotham*, 32.
175. Clute, *Annals of Staten Island*, 70.
176. Phillip Papas, *That Ever Loyal Island: Staten Island and the American Revolution* (New York: New York University Press, 2007), 112.
177. Shane White, "Slavery in New York State in the Early Republic," *Australasian Journal of American Studies* 14, no. 2 (December 1995): 1–29, 8.
178. Edna Holden, *Holden's Staten Island: The History of Richmond County: Revised Resource Manual Sketches for the Year Two Thousand Two*, ed. Richard B. Dickenson (New York: Center for Migration Studies, 2003), 476.
179. Edmund B. O'Callaghan, "Census of Slaves 1755 (Lower New York)," *Documentary History of the State of New-York; Arranged under the Direction of the Hon Christopher Morgan, Secretary of State*, vol. 3 (Albany, NY: Weed, Parsons & Company, 1850), 843–68, 867–68.
180. Ibid.
181. Bayles, *History of Richmond County*, 147–51.
182. White, "Slavery in New York State," 9.
183. "Bill of Sale for a Male Slave Named France," March 28, 1801, Perine Family Papers, online collections database of the Staten Island Historical Society, https://statenisland.pastperfectonline.com/archive/14D51416-87DA-44AF-B52E-099432225406.

184. James Gigantino, "Trading in Jersey Souls: New Jersey and the Interstate Slave Trade," *Pennsylvania History: A Journal of Mid-Atlantic Studies* 77, no. 3 (2010): 281–302, 286.
185. Thomas Hugh, *The Slave Trade: The Story of the Atlantic Slave Trade: 1440–1870* (New York: Simon and Schuster Paperbacks, 1997), 207. Interestingly, this also happened in reverse at other times, when traders wished to avoid Amboy's customs officials, as per Gigantino, "Trading in Jersey Souls," 287.
186. Larry A. Greene, "A History of Afro-Americans in New Jersey," *Journal of the Rutgers University Libraries* 56, no. 1 (1994): 4–71, 12.
187. Morris, *Morris's Memorial History of Staten Island*, 2:38–39. Incorrectly listed as "Tow Books."
188. James Guyon, *Town Book for Castletown for the Entry of Black Children, 1799–1827*, New-York Historical Society, New York, September 18, 1817, 24–25, image, http://digitalcollections.nyhistory.org/islandora/object/islandora%3A132011.
189. Leng and Davis, *Staten Island and Its People*, 1:212.
190. Morris, *Morris's Memorial History of Staten Island*, 2:39.
191. Ibid., 38–42.
192. Charles H. Wesley, "The Negroes of New York in the Emancipation Movement," *Journal of Negro History* 24, no. 1 (January 1939): 65–103, 68.
193. Leng and Davis, *Staten Island and Its People*, 1:236.
194. Morris, *Morris's Memorial History of Staten Island*, 2:46–47.
195. New York City Landmarks Preservation Commission, *565 and 569 Bloomingdale Road Cottages, 565 and 569 Bloomingdale Road, Staten Island, Built c. 1887 and 1898*, February 1, 2011, http://www.nyc.gov/html/records/pdf/govpub/5808baymens_cottages_sandy_ground.pdf.
196. Ibid.
197. Ibid.
198. William Askins, "Oysters and Equality: Nineteenth Century Cultural Resistance in Sandy Ground, Staten Island, New York," *Anthropology of Work Review* 12, no. 2 (June 1991): 7–13, 7–8.
199. Ibid.
200. New York City Landmarks Preservation Commission, *565 and 569 Bloomingdale Road Cottages*.
201. Robert L. Schuyler, "Sandy Ground: Archaeological Sampling in a Black Community in Metropolitan New York," *Conference on Historic Site Archaeology Papers* 7, part 2, ed. Stanley South, Conference on Historic

Site Archaeology, Institute of Archaeology and Anthropology, University of South Carolina (August 1974): 13–51, 47.

202. Tracey Porpora, "More than 500 Unmarked Graves Found in Community Settled by Freed Slaves," *Staten Island Advance*, July 11, 2016.

203. Debbie-Ann Paige, *National Parks Service: National Underground Railroad Network to Freedom Application: Louis Napoleon House c/o The Sandy Ground Historical Society*, July 1, 2011, https://www.academia.edu/3088830/NPS_UGRR_Louis_Napoleon_House_Site_Application.

204. Ibid.

205. Dale Baum and Dale T. Knobel, "Anatomy of a Realignment: New York Presidential Politics, 1848–1860," *New York History* 65, no. 1 (January 1984): 60–81, 62.

206. Ibid., 63.

207. Leng and Davis, *Staten Island and Its People*, 1:258.

208. Ibid., 482.

209. Ibid., 482–85.

210. Kenneth J. Zanca, "'Greater New York City Area Catholics': Participation in the Funeral of Abraham Lincoln," *New York History* 87, no. 2 (Spring 2006): 173–202, 176.

211. Leng and Davis, *Staten Island and Its People*, 2:757.

212. Debbie-Ann Paige, "Slow Burn: The Incendiary Politics of Race and Violence in Antislavery Conflict and the Effects on the Civil War Draft Riots in Richmond County, New York, 1855–1865," Master's thesis, The College of Staten Island/CUNY, 2012, 33.

213. Ibid., 37–38.

214. Leng and Davis, *Staten Island and Its People*, 1:259.

215. New York Public Library, NYPL Map Warper: Layer 869.

216. Vernon B. Hampton, *Staten Island's Claim to Fame: "The Garden Spot of New York Harbor"* (Staten Island, NY: Richmond Borough Pub. & Printing Company, circa 1925), 23.

217. Leng and Davis, *Staten Island and Its People*, 1:275.

218. Charles G. Hine and William T. Davis, *Legends, Stories and Folklore of Old Staten Island*, Part I, *The North Shore* (Staten Island, NY: Staten Island Historical Society, 1925), 65.

219. Paige, "Slow Burn," 45–47.

220. Ibid., 53–54. Paige cited an account from George L. Austin, *The Life and Times of Wendell Phillips* (Boston: Lee and Shepard Publishers, 1888).

221. Leng and Davis, *Staten Island and Its People*, 1:276.

222. Jon Grinspan, "'Young Men for War': The Wide Awakes and Lincoln's 1860 Presidential Campaign," in "Abraham Lincoln at 200: History and Historiography," special issue, *Journal of American History* 96, no. 2 (September 2009): 357–78, 357.

223. Ibid.

224. "The Wide Awake Organization, Their Origin and Progress," *New York Herald*, September 19, 1860.

225. "Mass Meeting," *Richmond County Gazette*, October 3, 1860.

226. "Richmond County Wide-Awakes," *Evening Post* (New York), September 27, 1860.

227. *Richmond County Gazette*, October 3, 1860, as quoted in Leng and Davis, *Staten Island and Its People*, 1:276.

228. Leng and Davis, *Staten Island and Its People*, 1:274–77.

229. D.T. Valentine, *Manual of the Corporation of the City of New York* (New York: Edmund Jones & Company, Printers, 1864), 164.

230. "The Official Vote," *Albany Journal* (Albany, NY), November 27, 1860.

231. Leng and Davis, *Staten Island and Its People*, 1:277.

232. Leo H. Hirsch Jr., "New York and the National Slavery Problem," *Journal of Negro History* 16, no. 4 (October 1931): 454–73, 472.

233. Tyler G. Anbinder, "Fernando Wood and New York City's Secession from the Union: A Political Reappraisal," *New York History* 68, no. 1 (January 1987): 66–92, 69–71.

234. Hirsch, "New York and the National Slavery Problem," 472.

235. Bayles, *History of Richmond County*, 274.

236. Ibid.

237. Ibid., 280.

238. Leng and Davis, *Staten Island and Its People*, 1:280.

239. Ibid., 281.

240. Ibid., 285.

241. Undated, quoted in Leng and Davis, *Staten Island and Its People*, 1:285.

242. Steinmeyer, *Staten Island*, 61.

243. "Volunteers Wanted at Once for the Eleventh Reg't (Stanton Legion), Now in Camp at New Dorp, Staten Island, Commanded by Colonel William H. Allen," 1861–65, New York Historical Society, New York, http://digitalcollections.nyhistory.org/islandora/object/islandora%3A159547.

244. "Camp New-Dorp and Sprague Barracks, Staten Island," *New York Times*, July 29, 1863.

245. A sample survey of the following two documents records deaths and dozens of desertions from Sprague Barracks in 1863: *Annual Report of the Adjutant-General of the State of New York for the Year 1898: Registers of the First, Second, Third, Fourth, Fifth and Fifth Veteran Infantry* (New York: Wynkoop Hallenbeck Crawford Company, State Printers, 1899), and *Annual Report of the Adjutant-General of the Staten of New York for the Year 1905: Registers of the One Hundred and Seventy-Eighth, One Hundred and Seventy-Ninth, One Hundred and Eightieth, One Hundred and Eighty-First, One Hundred and Eighty-Second, One Hundred and Eighty-Third, One Hundred and Eighty-Fourth, One Hundred and Eight-Fifth, One Hundred and Eighty Sixth and One Hundred and Eighty-Seventh Infantry* (Albany, NY: Brandow Printing Company, 1906).

246. "Richmond Co. Arouse! Town of Castleton in Particular! Now Is Your Time to Join a First-Rate Company in a First-Rate Richmond Co. Regiment, and Be Ready for the War in a Few Days," September 1, 1862, New York Historical Society, New York, http://ec2-35-169-86-46.compute-1.amazonaws.com/islandora/object/islandora%3A159514.

247. Leng and Davis, *Staten Island and Its People*, 1:293.

248. Todd A. Shallat, "American Gibraltars: Army Engineers and the Quest for a Scientific Defense of the Nation, 1815–1860," *Army History*, no. 66 (Winter 2008): 4–19, 6.

249. Emanuel R. Lewis, *Seacoast Fortifications of the United States: An Introductory History* (Novato, CA: Presidio, 1970), 56.

250. Leng and Davis, *Staten Island and Its People*, 1:279.

251. "Fort Richmond and Tompkins," *Richmond County Gazette*, May 7, 1862.

252. Morris, *Morris's Memorial History of Staten Island*, 2:387; Bayles, *History of Richmond County*, 274.

253. J. Barto Arnold, "Marine Magnetometer Survey of Archaeological Materials Near Galveston, Texas," *Historical Archaeology* 21, no. 1 (1987): 18–47, 26.

254. James Mooney, ed., *Dictionary of American Naval Fighting Ships*, vol. 1 (Washington, D.C.: Naval Historical Center, 1991), 407.

255. James Mooney, ed., *Dictionary of American Naval Fighting Ships*, vol. 6 (Washington, D.C.: Naval History Division, 1976), 74.

256. Maura Yates, "A Staten Island Ferry Goes to War: The Civil War–Era Tale of the USS Westfield," *Staten Island Advance*, December 27, 2009.

257. Gouverneur Morris, *The History of a Volunteer Regiment. Being a Succinct Account of the Organization, Services and Adventures of the Sixth Regiment New York Volunteers Infantry Known as Wilson Zouaves: Where They Went—What They Did—and What They Saw in the War of the Rebellion, 1861 to 1863* (New York: Veterans Volunteer Publishing Company, 1891), 25.

258. Alice S. Alexiou, *Devil's Mile: The Rich, Gritty History of the Bowery* (New York: St. Martin's Press, 2018), 118.

259. "Remarkable Exhibition of Savage—Wilson's Zouaves—Extraordinary Scenes," *Albany Journal*, May 26, 1861.

260. Bayles, *History of Richmond County*, 278.

261. Ibid.

262. Leng and Davis, *Staten Island and Its People*, 1:294.

263. Army of the Potomac, "General Orders No. 40. February 4, 1862," *General Orders and Index to the General Orders, 1861–1865*, part 1 (Washington, D.C.: Headquarters Printing Office, 1863), 12.

264. Bayles, *History of Richmond County*, 279.

265. "News of the Day. The War," *New York Tribune*, July 2, 1863.

266. "Notice," *New York Herald*, July 16, 1863.

267. "The Corcoran Legion; THE FIRST REGIMENT, THE SECOND REGIMENT, THE THIRD REGIMENT, THE FIFTH REGIMENT, THE SIXTH REGIMENT, THE SEVENTH REGIMENT, THE EIGHTH AND NINTH REGIMENTS," *New York Times*, September 13, 1862.

268. "Local News," *Richmond County Gazette*, November 12, 1862.

269. Ibid.

270. Morris, *Morris's Memorial History of Staten Island*, 2:398–99.

271. Leng and Davis, *Staten Island and Its People*, 1:293.

272. "Our Staten Island Boys at Bull Run," *Richmond County Gazette*, July 31, 1861.

273. Leng and Davis, *Staten Island and Its People*, 1:279.

274. Frederick Phisterer, *New York in the War of the Rebellion, 1861 to 1865*, vol. 5 (Albany, NY: J.B Lyon and Company, State Printers, 1912), 3,818 and 3,986.

275. *The Union Army: A History of Military Affairs in the Loyal States 1861–65, Records of the Regiments in the Union Army—Cyclopedia of Battles—Memoirs of Commanders and Soldiers*, vol. 2 (Madison, WI: Federal Publishing Company, 1908), 103–4.

276. Bayles, *History of Richmond County*, 302.

277. Phillip Papas, "Staten Island Memories: Island Awash in World War I Tributes," *Staten Island Advance*, May 19, 2013.

278. New York Monuments Commission for the Battlefields of Gettysburg and Chattanooga, *Final Report of the Battlefield of Gettysburg*, vol. 3 (Albany, NY: J.B. Lyon and Company Printers, 1900), 1,364.
279. Bob Raimonto, "150 Years On, Remembering a Staten Islander Whose Sacrifice Helped Stem the Rebel Tide at Gettysburg," *Staten Island Advance*, August 18, 2017.
280. New York Public Library, NYPL Map Warper: Layer 869.
281. New York Monuments Commission, 1,364.
282. Ibid.
283. Raimonto, "150 Years On."
284. Leng and Davis, *Staten Island and Its People*, 1:253.
285. Kenneth Finegold, *Experts and Politicians: Reform Challenges to Machine Politics in New York, Cleveland, and Chicago* (Princeton, NJ: Princeton University Press, 1995), 42.
286. Thomas Matteo, "Shaw Family Leaves Its Indelible Mark on Staten Island," *Staten Island Advance*, September 24, 2014.
287. Stephen T. Riley, "A Monument to Colonel Robert Gould Shaw," *Proceedings of the Massachusetts Historical Society*, Third Series, vol. 75 (1963): 27–38, 27–28.
288. Luis J. Emilio, *History of the Fifty-Fourth Regiment of Massachusetts Volunteer Infantry, 1863–1865* (Boston: Boston Book Company, 1894), 342.
289. Jason Daley, "Civil War Hero's Long-Lost Sword Was Hiding in an Attic," Smithsonian, https://www.smithsonianmag.com/smart-news/robert-gould-shaws-civil-war-sword-found-attic-180964076.
290. Riley, "Monument to Colonel Robert Gould Shaw," 29.
291. "Mayor Giuliani Signs Bill that Adds the Name 'Colonel Robert Gould Shaw's Glory Way' to Davis Avenue Between Richmond Terrace and Henderson Avenue on Staten Island," Archives of the Mayor's Press Office, October 7, 1998, http://www.nyc.gov/html/om/html/98b/pr470-98.html.
292. Albon P. Man Jr., "Labor Competition and the New York Draft Riots of 1863," *Journal of Negro History* 36, no. 4 (October 1951): 375–405, 376–79.
293. Albon P. Man Jr., "The Church and the New York Draft Riots of 1863," *Records of the American Catholic Historical Society of Philadelphia* 62, no. 1 (March 1951), 33–50, 35–36.
294. "City Politics. German Mayoralty Ratification Mass Meeting," *New York Herald*, November 28, 1861.

295. "THE CHARTER ELECTION; LISTS OF SUCCESSFUL CANDIDATES. GEORGE OPDYKE, MAYOR. Fernando Wood the Lowest in the Field. Scenes at the Various Political Headquarters. Excitement in and Around the Newspaper Offices. FOR MAYOR: COMPARATIVE VOTE BY WARDS. ALDERMEN ELECTED. THE VOTE FOR ALDERMEN. THE VOTE FOR COUNCILMEN. Police Justice for the Third Police Judicial District. SCHOOL COMMISSIONERS ELECTED," *New York Times*, December 4, 1861.
296. Burrows and Wallace, *Gotham*, 888.
297. Ibid., 888–95.
298. "Local News—The Draft," *Richmond County Gazette*, July 15, 1863.
299. Morris, *Morris's Memorial History of Staten Island*, 2:405–7.
300. *Annual Report of the Adjutant-General of the Staten of New York for the Year 1898: Registers of the Thirteenth and Fifteenth Regiments of Artillery* (New York: Wynkoop Hallenbeck Crawford Company, State Printers, 1898), 1–421.
301. *Annual Report of the Adjutant-General of the Staten of New York for the Year 1894*, vol. 4, *Registers of the 13th, 14th, 15th, 16th and 18th Regiments of Cavalry, N.Y. Vols., in War of the Rebellion* (Albany, NY: James B. Lyon, State Printers, 1895), 1–267.
302. Bayles, *History of Richmond County*, 311.
303. Ibid., 291.
304. Ibid., 292–93.
305. Ibid.; "Rioting on Staten Island," *Evening Post*, July 15, 1863.
306. Charles G. Hine, "The Riots of '63 on Staten Island," in *Legends, Stories, and Folklore*, 76–79, 78.
307. Ibid.; Charles E. Fitch, *Encyclopedia of Biography of New York: A Life Record of Men and Women of the Past* (New York: American Historical Society Inc., 1916), 26; "The Riots. No Renewal of the Riot this Afternoon. Threats of the Thieves. Workmen Resuming," *Evening Post*, July 16, 1863.
308. "Riot on Staten Island. The Depot Burned. Reported Riot in First Avenue," *Albany Journal*, July 16, 1863.
309. Bayles, *History of Richmond County*, 293.
310. "Movements of the Military. Organization for Home Protection," *New York Herald*, July 16, 1863.
311. Martin Gay, "A Child's Recollection of the Draft Riots," in *Legends, Stories, and Folklore*, 69–76, 74–75.
312. Bayles, *History of Richmond County*, 295.
313. "Staten Island," *New York Herald*, July 19, 1863.

314. Frederick Phisterer, *New York in the War of the Rebellion*, vol. 1 (Albany, NY: Weed, Parsons & Company, 1890), 383.

315. "Riotous Proceedings on Staten Island. Two Men Killed—Several Persons Wounded. The Mob Dispersed—Twenty-Four Prisoners Taken," *Evening Post*, July 21, 1863.

316. Ibid.

317. "Affray on Staten Island. Two Men Killed—Several Persons Wounded," *New York Daily Tribune*, July 22, 1863.

318. "Local News—Fatal Monday Melee Near Vanderbilt Landing," *Richmond County Gazette*, July 22, 1863; Bayles, *History of Richmond County*, 295.

319. "Affray on Staten Island."

320. "Riotous Proceedings on Staten Island."

321. "Affray on Staten Island."

322. Ibid.

323. *Annual Report of the Adjutant-General of the State of New York for the Year 1900: The Twelfth, Thirteenth, Fourteenth, Sixteenth, Seventeenth, Seventeenth Veteran, and Eighteenth Regiments of Infantry*, vol. 19 (Albany, NY: J.B Lyon, State Printers, 1900), 844.

324. "The Troubles on Staten Island," *New York Herald*, July 24, 1863.

325. Ibid.

326. Ibid.

327. James Carson, *Chasing Mosby, Killing Booth: The 16ᵗʰ New York Volunteer Cavalry* (Jefferson, NC: McFarland and Company, Publishers, 2017), 34.

328. "Staten Island; THE LATE INCENDIARY FIRE AT CAMP NEW DORP, SPRAGUE BARRACKS THE EXTENT OF THE CONFLAGRATION CREDITABLE EXERTIONS OF COLLAPSING, THE OFFICERS AND SOLDIERS PRESENT APPEARANCES OF THE BARRACKS THE INCENDIARY STILL UNDISCOVERED," *New York Times*, August 15, 1863.

329. "New York, State Census, 1855," database online, Ancestry.com, original data: Census of the State of New York, for 1855, microfilm, various county clerk offices, New York.

330. Morris, *Morris's Memorial History of Staten Island*, 2:396.

Chapter 3

331. Social Explorer, "US Demography 1790 to Present," https://www.socialexplorer.com/a9676d974c/explore.

332. Leng and Davis, *Staten Island and Its People*, 1:288.
333. Ibid.
334. Ibid., 2:354–55; Bayles, *History of Richmond County*, 330.
335. "AN ACT to Appoint Commissioners to Prepare and Submit a Plan for Roads, Avenues, Parks and Other Improvements on Staten Island, and for Improvement of the Means of Communication to and from Said Island. Passed May 5, 1870; Three-Fifths Being Present," chapter 627, *Laws of New York Passed at the Ninety-Third Session of the Legislature, Begun January Fourth, and Ended April Twenty-Sixth, 1870, in the City of Albany*," vol. 2 (Albany, NY: Weed, Parsons and Company, Printers, 1870), 1,458.
336. Ibid.
337. Edwin Williams, *The New-York Annual Register for the Year of Our Lord 1833: Containing an Almanac, Civil and Judicial List; with Political, Statistical, and Other Information, Respecting the State of New-York and the United States* (New York: Peter Hill, 1833), 227.
338. James G. Wilson and John Fiske, eds., *Appletons' Cyclopedia of American Biography*, vol. 5, Pickering-Sumter (New York: D. Appleton and Company, 1900), 318.
339. Beau Riffenburgh, "James Gordon Bennett, the New York Herald and the Arctic," *Polar Record* 27, no. 160 (1991): 9–16.
340. "AN ACT to Appoint Commissioners," 1,458.
341. "Andrew H. Green's Busy Life," *New York Times*, November 14, 1903.
342. "Andrew H. Green and Central Park," *New York Times*, October 10, 1897.
343. Staten Island Improvement Commission, *Report of a Preliminary Scheme of Improvements* (New York: James Sutton Company, Printers and Stationers, 1871), 96.
344. Ibid., 28.
345. Ibid., 78 and 87.
346. Ibid., 66.
347. Ibid., 68.
348. Ibid., 71.
349. Ibid., 94.
350. Ibid., 28.
351. Ibid., 76.
352. Leng and Davis, *Staten Island and Its People*, 1:305.
353. "The Westfield Disaster. Graphic Accounts by Eye-Witnesses. The Dead and Dying at Bellevue Hospital. Four More Bodies Found in the Water," *Evening Post*, July 31, 1871.

354. Ibid.

355. "Sunday's Slaughter Further Details of the Westfield Woe Death of Two More of the Victims the Total—Ninety-Three," *New York Herald*, August 3, 1871.

356. "The Conclusion of the Westfield Inquest a Righteous Verdict," *New York Herald*, August 17, 1871.

357. Leng and Davis, *Staten Island and Its People*, 2:696.

358. Ibid., 693–94.

359. "The New Ferry Bill," *Richmond County Gazette*, February 25, 1863.

360. *Journal of the Assembly of the State of New York: At Their Eighty-Sixth Session, Begun and Held at the Capitol, in the City of Albany, on the Sixth Day of January, 1863* (Albany, NY: Comstock & Cassidy, 1863), 295.

361. Ibid., 561.

362. Leng and Davis, *Staten Island and Its People*, 2:695.

363. Ibid., 698.

364. "For Sale," *New-York and Richmond County Free Press*, May 11, 1833.

365. Leng and Davis, *Staten Island and Its People*, 2:698–99.

366. Ibid., 701–2.

367. Brian J. Cudahy, *Over and Back: The History of Ferryboats in New York Harbor* (New York: Fordham University Press, 1990), 122.

368. Ibid., 705–6.

369. Shepherd, *Tottenville*, 78.

370. Morris, *Morris's Memorial History of Staten Island*, 2:462.

371. David Goldfarb and James G. Ferreri, *St. George* (Charleston, SC: Arcadia Publishing, 2009), 8.

372. Bayles, *History of Richmond County*, 691.

373. Morris, *Morris's Memorial History of Staten Island*, 2:463.

374. Ibid.

375. "Important Movement," *Commercial Advertiser*, June 6, 1860.

376. Bayles, *History of Richmond County*, 671.

377. "Local News," *Richmond County Gazette*, November 27, 1867.

378. Leng and Davis, *Staten Island and Its People*, 2:717–18.

379. Ibid.

380. New York Public Library, NYPL Map Warper: Layer 869.

381. Leng and Davis, *Staten Island and Its People*, 2:717.

382. New York Public Library, NYPL Map Warper: Layer 1035, *Atlas of the City of New York, Borough of Richmond. From Actual Surveys and Original Plans, by George W. and Walter S. Bromley.*

383. "Rapid Transit on Staten Island," *New York Times*, January 17, 1886.

384. Morris, *Morris's Memorial History of Staten Island*, 2:465.

385. Edward F. Bommer, "The Baltimore and Ohio Railroad in New Jersey," Jersey Central Railroad Historical Society Chapter of the National Railroad Historical Society, July 3, 2004, http://jcrhs.org/B&O.html.

386. "The Largest Drawbridge. Completion of the Big Span Across the Arthur Kill," *New York Times*, June 14, 1888.

387. "State Wedded Unto State. Imperial New York Leads New Jersey, an Unwilling Bride to the Altar," *Richmond County Gazette*, June 20, 1888.

388. Bommer, "Baltimore and Ohio Railroad in New Jersey."

389. "State Wedded Unto State."

390. H. Bartlett Novelty Company, "Picturesque Staten Island," 1886, Online Collections Database of the Staten Island Historical Society, July 2016, https://statenisland.pastperfectonline.com/webobject/F0C059D5-3007-44BD-A3A9-791145190600.

391. Leng and Davis, *Staten Island and Its People*, 1:319.

392. Harold Seymour, *Baseball: The Early Years* (New York: Oxford University Press, 1960), 214.

393. H. Bartlett Novelty Company, "Picturesque Staten Island," 1886; quoted in William I. Roberts et al., Greenhouse Consultants Inc., *Phase IA Historical/Archaeological Sensitivity Evaluation of the St. George Railyard Project Staten Island, New York*, May 14, 1987, revised March 1989, New York City Landmarks Preservation Commission, http://s-media.nyc.gov/agencies/lpc/arch_reports/634.pdf, 10.

394. Leng and Davis, *Staten Island and Its People*, 1:319.

395. Ibid.

396. Erastus Wiman, *Chances of Success: Episodes and Observations in the Life of a Busy Man* (Toronto: American Book Company, 1893), 166–67.

397. Ibid., 167.

398. Buffalo Bill's Museum and Grave, "Did Buffalo Bill Visit Your Town? A Comprehensive County/State Listing of William 'Buffalo Bill' Cody's Tour Destinations," http://www.buffalobill.org/pdfs/buffalo_bill_visits.pdf.

399. Wiman, *Chances of Success*, 167.

400. Andrew Wilson, "Found Staten Island Stories 3: Buffalo Bill's Wild West, Mariners Harbor, 1886 and 1888," New York Public Library, September 23, 2016, https://www.nypl.org/blog/2016/09/23/clone-found-staten-island-stories-3-buffalo-bills-wild-west-mariners-harbor-1886-and.

401. Wiman, *Chances of Success*, 167.

402. "S.I. Amusement Grounds," *Richmond County Advance*, June 12, 1886.

403. "Many Happy People," *New York Herald*, June 29, 1886.
404. "Mariners Harbor," *Richmond County Advance*, July 24, 1886.
405. Advertisement, *New York Herald*, February 13, 1887.
406. Advertisement, *New York Tribune*, May 13, 1887.
407. Advertisement, *New York Herald*, May 12, 1887.
408. Social Explorer, "US Demography 1790 to Present."
409. "New York in 1834: Amusements and Places of Recreation," *Dublin Penny Journal* 3, no. 116 (September 20, 1834): 90–91, 90.
410. Kenneth T. Jackson, ed., *The Encyclopedia of New York*, 2nd ed. (New Haven, CT: Yale University Press, 2010), 1,213.
411. New York Public Library, NYPL Map Warper: Layer 869.
412. "Staten Island in the Spring. The Westchester Walking Club Again on the Road—Salt Air and Rural Scenes," *New York Herald*, May 12, 1879.
413. Jackson, *Encyclopedia of New York*, 889.
414. New York Public Library, NYPL Map Warper: Layer 869.
415. Vera Haller, "Westerleigh, S.I., Built on Temperance," *New York Times*, April 8, 2014.
416. Leng and Davis, *Staten Island and Its People*, 2:718.
417. "Staten Island Happenings," *New York Tribune*, August 31, 1896.
418. "Staten Island Happenings," *New York Tribune*, June 1, 1897.
419. "Trolley Cars Crowded," *Richmond County Advance*, August 1, 1896.
420. "Staten Island Happenings," *New York Tribune*, July 5, 1897.
421. Jackson, *Encyclopedia of New York*, 839.
422. "Soldiers on the Rampage," *Richmond County Advance*, August 29, 1900.
423. Ibid.
424. Leng and Davis, *Staten Island and Its People*, 2:631.
425. New York Public Library, NYPL Map Warper: Layer 1035.
426. Leng and Davis, *Staten Island and Its People*, 2:631.
427. "Staten Island Happenings," *New York Tribune*, August 31, 1896.
428. *Illustrated Sketch Book of Staten Island, New York, Its Industries and Commerce* (New York: S.C. Judson, 1886), 158.
429. Advertisement, "The Woods of Arden," *New York Tribune*, July 25, 1885.
430. *Illustrated Sketch Book of Staten Island*, 158.
431. Staten Island Cricket Club, "A Brief History," https://www.statenislandcc.org/history.
432. George B. Kirsch, "American Cricket: Players and Clubs Before the Civil War," *Journal of Sport History* 11, no. 1 (Spring 1984): 28–50 42.
433. "Cricket on Staten Island," *New York Times*, June 24, 1877.
434. "Games of Cricket," *New York Times*, July 6, 1886.

435. *1880 United States Federal Census*, database online, Ancestry.com.
436. Amisha Padnani, "Overlooked: Mary Ewing Outerbridge," *New York Times*, March 9, 2018.
437. E.M Hallliday, "Sphairistiké, Anyone?" *American Heritage* 22, no. 4 (June 1971), https://www.americanheritage.com/content/sphairistiké-anyone.
438. Padnani, "Overlooked."
439. Ibid.
440. International Tennis Hall of Fame, "Mary Outerbridge," https://www.tennisfame.com/hall-of-famers/inductees/mary-outerbridge.
441. *Illustrated Sketch Book of Staten Island*, 99.
442. Ibid.
443. Bayles, *History of Richmond County*, 726.
444. Ibid., 729–30.
445. New York Public Library, NYPL Map Warper: Layer 869.
446. "Railway News. A Conflagration on Staten Island. Destruction of Mayer and Bachman's Large Brewery at Clifton—the Loss Nearly $500,000," *New York Tribune*, November 1, 1881.
447. Bayles, *History of Richmond County*, 731.
448. Patricia M. Salmon, "Staten Island Memories: The Business of Brewing," *Staten Island Advance*, December 16, 2012.
449. Bayles, *History of Richmond County*, 727.
450. *Illustrated Sketch Book of Staten Island*, 100.
451. Ibid.
452. Ibid.
453. "Present Condition of Ireland," *Christian Examiner and Religious Miscellany* 45, Fourth Series, vol. 10 (July 1848): 114.
454. Margaret Lundrigan, *Irish Staten Island* (Charleston, SC: Arcadia Publishing, 2009), 10.
455. Edna Ishayik, "Refugees of Irish Famine to Get Proper Burial," *New York Times*, April 25, 2014.
456. Edward J. Lenik and Nancy L. Gibbs, *Topic-Intensive Research: Supplementary Historical Resources Investigation and Core Sample Analysis of the Staten Island Criminal Court and Family Court Complex Site, Staten Island New York*, Dormitory Authority of the State of New York, February 2001, 6.
457. Michael Vigorito, "The Quarantine Grounds and Hospitals," *The Watering Place* (blog), Seton Hall University Digital Humanities Project, June 26, 2016, https://blogs.shu.edu/mvdh/the-watering-place/quarntine-grounds-and-hospitals.

458. Ishayik, "Refugees of Irish Famine to Get Proper Burial."
459. Ibid.
460. Morris, *Morris's Memorial History of Staten Island*, 2:386.
461. Carolee Inskeep, *The Graveyard Shift: A Family Historian's Guide to New York City Cemeteries* (Orem, UT: Ancestry Publishing, 2000), 143.
462. Edward J. Lenik and Nancy L. Gibbs, *Phase 1A Cultural Resources Investigation for the Staten Island Criminal Court Complex, Staten Island, New York*, Dormitory Authority of the State of New York, November 2000, 16.
463. Edward J. Lenik and Nancy L. Gibbs, *Topic-Intensive Research: Supplementary Historical Resources Investigation and Core Sample Analysis of the Staten Island Criminal Court and Family Court Complex Site, Staten Island New York*, Dormitory Authority of the State of New York, February 2001, 6–8.
464. Ibid.
465. New York Public Library, NYPL Map Warper: Layer 869.
466. Ibid., Layer 1035.
467. Sergey Kadinsky, *Hidden Waters of New York City: A History and Guide to 101 Forgotten Lakes* (New York: Countryman Press, 2016), 86.
468. Leng and Davis, *Staten Island and Its People*, 1:332.
469. Daniel C. Kramer and Richard M. Flanagan, *Staten Island: Conservative Bastion in a Liberal City* (Lanham, MD: University Press of America, 2012), 28.
470. Ibid., 18.
471. Leng and Davis, *Staten Island and Its People*, 3:22.
472. Ibid., 1:353, 2:548.
473. Ibid., 3:303.
474. Margaret Lundrigan and Tova Navarra, *Staten Island in the Twentieth Century* (Charleston, SC: Arcadia Publishing, 1998), 20.
475. *1930 United States Federal Census*, database online, Ancestry.com.
476. Leng and Davis, *Staten Island and Its People*, 4:514.
477. "Injured by Trolley," *Richmond County Advance*, November 15, 1902.
478. "Funeral of Joseph Johnson," *Richmond County Advance*, November 22, 1902.
479. Bayles, *History of Richmond County*, 486.
480. Ibid., 482.
481. Leng and Davis, *Staten Island and Its People*, 2:822.
482. "Captain Burke, Civil War Vet, Is Dead at 92," *Staten Island Advance*, April 24, 1928.

483. Jeremiah O'Donovan Rossa, *Rossa's Recollections. 1838 to 1898* (Mariner's Harbor, NY: O'Donovan Rossa, 1898), 378.

484. Leng and Davis, *Staten Island and Its People*, 2:822.

485. "O'Donovan Rossa's Mission to Ireland: On His Way to Unveil a Monument to the Manchester Martyrs," *Irish World* (New York), November 19, 1904.

486. "O'Donovan Rossa's Funeral. Scenes in Dublin. Speech at Graveside," *Irish Times* (Dublin), August 2, 1915.

487. Patrick J. Hayes, "Father Drumgoole's Catechetical Playland: Education as Refuge in Nineteenth-Century New York," *American Catholic Studies* 123, no. 1 (Spring 2012): 25–49, 26.

488. Ibid., 26–32.

489. "Father Drumgoole Honored," *New York Times*, April 16, 1894.

490. Hayes, "Father Drumgoole's Catechetical Playland," 37–39.

491. "Father Drumgoole Honored."

492. "Mount Loretto," *Donohoe's Magazine* 36, no. 4 (October 1896): 421.

493. "We Get It at Last," *Wall Street Daily News*, March 14, 1888.

494. Hayes, "Father Drumgoole's Catechetical Playland," 46.

495. "Death of Father Drumgoole," *New York Times*, March 30, 1888.

Chapter 4

496. John Foord, *The Life and Public Services of Andrew Haswell Green* (Garden City, NY: Doubleday, Page & Company, 1913), 178.

497. *Report of the Committee on Incorporation of Cities and Villages on the Bill Relative to the Metropolitan Police Law. Transmitted to the Legislature February 17, 1858* (Albany, NY: C. Van Benthuysen, Printer to the Legislature, 1858), 3.

498. Foord, *Life and Public Services of Andrew Haswell Green*, 179.

499. Barry J. Kaplan, "Andrew H. Green and the Creation of a Planning Rationale: The Formation of Greater New York City, 1865–1890," *Urbanism Past & Present*, no. 8 (Summer 1979), 32–41, 33–34.

500. "A Spring Jaunt in Staten Island," *Harper's New Monthly Magazine* 57, no. 340 (September 1878): 545–57, 545.

501. Charles L. Brace, *The Dangerous Classes of New York, and Twenty Years' Work Among Them* (New York: Wynkoop & Hallenbeck, Publishers, 1872), 86–87.

502. Leng and Davis, *Staten Island and Its People*, 2:595.

503. Art and Picture Collection, New York Public Library, "Summer Resort of the Children's Aid Society on Staten Island," New York Public Library Digital Collections, http://digitalcollections.nypl.org/items/510d47e1-2876-a3d9-e040-e00a18064a99.
504. Kristy L. Slominsky, "YMCA, YWCA," in *Encyclopedia of Global Religion*, vol. 1, eds. Mark Juergensmeyer and Wade C. Roof (Los Angeles, CA: Sage Publication, 2012), 1,395.
505. *Illustrated Sketch Book of Staten Island*, 25; Leng and Davis, *Staten Island and Its People*, 2:597.
506. *Illustrated Sketch Book of Staten Island*, 25.
507. Leng and Davis, *Staten Island and Its People*, 2:598–99.
508. *Illustrated Sketch Book of Staten Island*, 27–30; Leng and Davis, *Staten Island and Its People*, 2:581.
509. *Illustrated Sketch Book of Staten Island*, 25.
510. Clute, *Annals of Staten Island*, 250.
511. James Ferreri, "Once Upon a Time, There Was a 'Castle,'" *Staten Island Advance*, March 10, 2012.
512. Leng and Davis, *Staten Island and Its People*, 2:578.
513. Ferreri, "Once Upon a Time, There Was a 'Castle.'"
514. Seamen's Society for Children and Families, "Our History," http://seamenssociety.org/history-of-sscf.
515. Ibid.; Bayles, *History of Richmond County*, 645.
516. Leng and Davis, *Staten Island and Its People*, 2:592.
517. *Copy of the Last Will and Testament of the Late Robert Richard Randall, Esq. of The Act of Incorporation, and of the Other Acts of the Legislature of the State of New-York, Respecting the Sailors' Snug Harbor: Together with the Names of the Persons Who Have Acted as Trustees of the Same—with Their By-Laws, &c.* (New York: Robert Carter, 1848), 5.
518. Barnett Shepherd, "Sailors' Snug Harbor Reattributed to Minard Lafever," *Journal of the Society of Architectural Historians* 35, no. 2 (May 1976): 108–23, 108–9.
519. "Local Miscellany. Judge Van Brunt Not Reappointed. Judge Beach Selected in His Place to Assist," *New York Tribune*, January 3, 1880.
520. *Illustrated Sketch Book of Staten Island*, 90.
521. Ibid.
522. Ibid.
523. Kaplan, "Andrew H. Green," 34.
524. "Staten Island's Snug Machine. Tammany Methods Imported into Richmond County Have Worked," *New York Herald*, January 8, 1894.

525. "Nicholas Muller," *A Biographical Congressional Directory: 1774 to 1903* (Washington: Government Printing Office, 1903). 710.

526. "Staten Island's Snug Machine."

527. "No Room for Democrats at Sailor's Snug Harbor. Veteran Tars Expelled from the Institution for Political Reasons," *New York Herald*, June 7, 1889.

528. Ibid.

529. Ibid.

530. "Immolated for Their Politics. The Half Has Not Been Told of Governor Trask's Methods," *New York Herald*, June 8, 1889.

531. "The Herald Saved His Life. Governor Trask, of Sailors' Snug Habor, Would Have Been a Dead Man If He Hadn't Had a Copy in His Pocket," *New York Herald*, December 8, 1889.

532. "Autocrat Trask. How He Treated Captain Childs at the Sailors' Snug Harbor," *New York Herald*, March 14, 1890.

533. "Snug Harbor," *New York Herald*, March 31, 1890.

534. "Vindicating Capt. Trask. Re-Elected Governor of Sailors' Snug Harbor. Resolutions Passed Endorsing His Official Conduct," *New York Herald*, April 1, 1890.

535. "Other Suburban Towns. Westchester County. Topics Before the Teachers' Institute," *New York Tribune*, May 7, 1890.

536. "Sentenced Election Inspectors. Richmond County Men Get Both Imprisonment and Fines," *New York Herald*, June 5, 1894.

537. "Don't Cheat! It Didn't Pay Very Well at the Last Election, and Will Not Pay at All This Year—Read What Happened to Men Who Cheated Last Fall," *Staten Island Independent*, October 26, 1894.

538. "The Snugs Can't Vote," *Richmond County Advance*, November 2, 1894.

539. "The Prostitution of Our Police Force," *Staten Island Independent*, October 26, 1894.

540. "The Chances of Success," *Staten Island Independent*, October 26, 1894.

541. "All Sorts," *Staten Island Independent*, April 12, 1895.

542. "Consolidation: What Port Richmond's Businessmen Think of It," *Staten Island Independent*, November 23, 1894.

543. Ibid.

544. Staten Island Improvement Commission, 21–22.

545. A.T. Andreas, *History of Chicago: From the Earliest Period to the Present Time*, vol. 2, *From 1857 Until the fire of 1871* (Chicago: A.T. Andreas Company, 1885), 49.

NOTES TO PAGES 106–109

546. "Staten Island's Future: Vast Schemes for Development Now Under Way," *New York Times*, May 10, 1896.
547. Howard P. Chudacoff, Judith E. Smith and Peter C. Baldwin, *The Evolution of American Urban History*, 8th ed. (New York: Routledge, 2016), 90.
548. Burrows and Wallace, *Gotham*, 1,223.
549. David M. Scobey, *Empire City: The Making and Meaning of the New York City Landscape* (Philadelphia, PA: Temple University Press, 2002), 265.
551. Michael P. McCarthy, "The Philadelphia Consolidation of 1854: A Reappraisal," *Pennsylvania Magazine of History and Biography* 110, no. 4 (October 1986): 531–48, 531.
552. Social Explorer, "US Demography 1790 to Present."
553. Edward C. Graves, *The Greater New York, Reasons Why: Consolidation Pamphlet No. 2* (New York: H.A. Rost, Printer, 1894), 15.
554. Social Explorer, "US Demography 1790 to Present."
555. Hammack, *Power and Society: Greater New York at the Turn of the Century* (New York: Columbia University Press, 1987), 194–96.
556. Andrew H. Green and the Commission of Municipal Consolidation Inquiry, *Communication of Andrew H. Green to the Legislature of the State of New York*, March 4, 1890, in Andrew H. Green, *New York of the Future: Writings and Addresses by Andrew H. Green* (New York: Stettiner, Lambert & Company, 1893), 20.
557. Ibid., 22.
558. Hammack, *Power and Society*, 195–96.
559. Green, *Communication of Andrew H. Green to the Legislature*, 24.
560. Ibid., 23.
561. *In the Court of Appeals of the State of New York. Albany County Savings Bank, Respondent, Against Thomas McCarty, Mary McCarty and Others, Appellants* (Albany, NY: Argus Company, Printers, 1894), 42.
562. New York Public Library, NYPL Map Warper: Layer 1035.
563. Alexander R. Smith, ed., "Lamentable Death of A.B. Pouch," *Port of New York Harbor and Marine Review* 2, no. 1 (January 1923): 28.
564. Bayles, *History of Richmond County*, 705–6.
565. William T. Davis and Charles W. Leng, *Staten Island Names: Ye Olde Names and Nicknames* (New Brighton, PA: Natural Science Association, 1896), 57.
566. Pamela H. Simpson, "Democratic Coverings for Floors and Walls," *Perspectives in Vernacular Architecture* 7 (1997): 281–92, 281–82.

567. Bayles, *History of Richmond County*, 721.
568. New York Public Library, NYPL Map Warper: Layer 869.
569. Ibid.
570. Bayles, *History of Richmond County*, 724–25.
571. *Illustrated Sketch Book of Staten Island*, 30 and 49.
572. Martha Joanna Lamb, *History of the City of New York: Its Origin, Rise, and Progress* (New York: A.S. Barnes, 1877), 726.
573. Brooke Blades and Michael Tomkins, *A Phase IA Archaeological Survey for the Arthur Kill Factory Outlet Center, Staten Island, Borough of Richmond, Richmond County, New York City, New York*, prepared for Bellemead Development Corporation, June 1995, http://s-media.nyc.gov/agencies/lpc/arch_reports/748.pdf.
574. George William Sheldon, *The Story of the Volunteer Fire Department of the City of New York* (New York: Harper Brothers, 1882), 194.
575. "From the Corsair. Staten Island," *Richmond County Mirror*, July 20, 1839.
576. Ibid.
577. Lionel Pincus and Princess Firyal Map Division, New York Public Library, *Map of Staten Island or Richmond County, N.Y.*, New York Public Library Digital Collection, http://digitalcollections.nypl.org/items/bb112759-d5d6-5e42-e040-e00a1806410f.
578. New York Public Library, NYPL Map Warper: Layer 869.
579. Ibid.
580. Andrew S. Dolkart and Mathew A. Postal, New York City Landmarks Preservation Commission, *Guide to New York City Landmarks*, 4th ed. (New York: John Wiley & Sons Inc., 2009), 390.
581. "Suicide of the Wealthy Man. Edward B. Kreischer, without Apparent Reason, Ends His Life with a Bullet," *New York Herald*, June 9, 1894.
582. Bayles, *History of Richmond County*, 732–33.
583. Dolkart and Postal, *Guide to New York City Landmarks*, 389–90.
584. Bayles, *History of Richmond County*, 736.
585. Leng and Davis, *Staten Island and Its People*, 2:911.
586. Ibid., 1:312.
587. "From Prince's Bay, S.S. White Was Supplying the World's Dental Needs," *Staten Island Advance*, May 27, 2011.
588. Leng and Davis, *Staten Island and Its People*, 2:950.
589. Year: *1860*, Census Place: *Westfield, Richmond, New York*, Roll: *M653_850*, Page: *177*, Family History Library Film: *803850, 1860*

United States Federal Census, database online, Ancestry.com, images reproduced by FamilySearch.

590. New York Public Library, NYPL Map Warper: Layer 869.

591. Bayles, *History of Richmond County*, 738–40; "From Prince's Bay, S.S. White."

592. Holden, *Holden's Staten Island*, 121.

593. Ibid.

594. New York Public Library, NYPL Map Warper: Layer 1035.

595. U.S., Alien Property Custodian, *Annual Report of the Alien Property Custodian* (Washington, D.C.: Government Printing Office, 1919), 325 and 562.

596. Ibid., 218.

597. "The Ice Business Once Flourished Here," *Staten Island Advance*, December 19, 2010.

598. Advertisement, *Staten Island Advance*, November 3, 1894.

599. Ibid.

600. Andrew H. Green, *At a Meeting of the Commissioners, Held December 11, 1890, at the Office of the President*, December 11, 1890, in Andrew H. Green, *New York of the Future: Writings and Addresses by Andrew H. Green* (New York: Stettiner, Lambert & Company, 1893), 55.

601. "Consolidation: What Port Richmond's Businessmen Think of It," *Staten Island Independent*, November 23, 1894.

602. Ibid.

603. Ibid.

604. Bayles, *History of Richmond County*, 449.

605. Leng and Davis, *Staten Island and Its People*, 1:504.

606. Ibid.

607. Bayles, *History of Richmond County*, 450.

608. Leng and Davis, *Staten Island and Its People*, 1:523.

609. "Public Library on Staten Island," *Richmond County Advance*, May 19, 1894.

610. Leng and Davis, *Staten Island and Its People*, 1:523.

611. *Illustrated Sketch Book of Staten Island*, 20.

612. New York State Water Supply Commission, *Annual Report of the State Water Supply* (Albany, NY: Brandow Printing Company, 1906), 130.

613. Ibid.

614. Arthur Hollick, "Our Water Supply," *Proceedings of the Natural Science Association of Staten Island* 4, no. 14 (February 9, 1895): 61.

615. Davis and Leng, *Staten Island Names*, 47 and 53.

616. Holden, *Holden's Staten Island*, 127.
617. Leng and Davis, *Staten Island and Its People*, 1:271.
618. *Illustrated Sketch Book of Staten Island*, 96.
619. Ibid.; Leng and Davis, *Staten Island and Its People*, 1:271.
620. Bayles, *History of Richmond County*, 235.
621. *Illustrated Sketch Book of Staten Island*, 96.
622. Leng and Davis, *Staten Island and Its People*, 1:271.
623. Shepherd, *Tottenville*, 117.
624. Leng and Davis, *Staten Island and Its People*, 1:305.
625. A.E. Costello, *Our Police Protectors: History of the New York Police from the Earliest Period to the Present Time* (New York: published by the author, 1885), 138, 188 and 234.
626. Ibid., 146.
627. "THE METROPOLITAN POLICE MACHINE; The Old Police of the 'Bloody Sixth' Contrasted with the Existing Force. EXTRACTS FROM POLICE LAWS. Police Life-Insurance Fund the School of Instruction Military Drill. LOST CHILDREN RESTORED. The Detective Force, the Police Telegraph, and the Sanitary Squad. Names of Officers of Precincts, Statistics, etc. CERTAIN RULES UNDER WHICH THE POLICE ARE GOVERNED. POLICE SCHOOL OF INSTRUCTION. MILITARY DRILL. POLICEMEN'S DUTIES. LOST CHILDREN. OTHER APARTMENTS AT HEADQUARTERS. OFFICE OF THE DETECTIVE POLICE, THE ROGUES' GALLERY THE POLICE TELEGRAPH. THE EDIFICE. COMPOSITION OF THE FORCE. MONTHLY DAY OFF. PATRIOTISM OF THE FORCE. COST OF THE INSTITUTION, AND HOW IT COULD BE RENDERED MORE USEFUL," *New York Times*, May 14, 1865.
628. Costello, *Our Police Protectors*, 139.
629. John Kleinig and Yurong Zhang, *Professional Law Enforcement Codes: A Documentary Collection* (Westport, CT: Greenwood Press, 1993), 55–56.
630. Leng and Davis, *Staten Island and Its People*, 1:306.
631. *Illustrated Sketch Book of Staten Island*, 24.
632. Graves, *Greater New York*, 24.
633. "Consolidation: What Port Richmond's Businessmen Think of It," *Staten Island Independent*, November 23, 1894.
634. Arthur W. Dean, letter to the editor, *Staten Island Advance*, August 15, 1891.
635. Ibid.
636. Amy S. Greenberg, *Cause for Alarm: The Volunteer Fire Department in the Nineteenth Century* (Princeton, NJ: Princeton University Press, 1998), 111.
637. Leng and Davis, *Staten Island and Its People*, 1:250.
638. Ibid., 2:778–79.

639. Shepherd, *Tottenville*, 138.
640. "Went Up in Smoke: One Thousand Dollars Worth of Fireworks Destroyed," *Staten Island Independent*, June 14, 1895.
641. Leng and Davis, *Staten Island and Its People*, 2:778.
642. *Illustrated Sketch Book of Staten Island*, 20.
643. Leng and Davis, *Staten Island and Its People*, 2:778.
644. *Illustrated Sketch Book of Staten Island*, 20.

Chapter 5

645. Morris, *Morris's Memorial History of Staten Island*, 2:408.
646. "Richmond County's Fete. The Bicentennial Anniversary to Be Celebrated with Much Pageantry," *New York Herald*, November 1, 1883.
647. "Staten Island Awake. Celebrating the Bicentennial of Richmond County," *New York Herald*, November 2, 1883.
648. Ibid.
649. Ibid.
650. Morris, *Morris's Memorial History of Staten Island*, 2:411.
651. Burrows and Wallace, *Gotham*, 1,221–22.
652. Hammack, *Power and Society*, 192–93.
653. Leng and Davis, *Staten Island and Its People*, 3:18–19.
654. David J. Tysen, *Happenings Before and After Staten Island Became Part of Greater New York* (Staten Island, NY: Staten Island Chamber of Commerce, 1924), 12.
655. Albert Shaw, *The Life of Col. Geo. E. Waring, Jr., the Greatest Apostle of Cleanliness* (New York: Patriot League, 1899), 13–14, 33.
656. Tysen, *Happenings Before and After*, 12.
657. Ibid.
658. "The Metropolis of the Future," *New York Herald*, March 17, 1889.
659. "Death of E.H. Crosby. Social Reformer Was Stricken with Pneumonia in Baltimore," *New York Times*, January 4, 1907.
660. Hammack, *Power and Society*, 193–94.
661. Leng and Davis, *Staten Island and Its People*, 2:420.
662. "Veteran Editor Gone. Erastus Brooks Dead at His Staten Island Home," *New York Times*, November 26, 1886.
663. Leng and Davis, *Staten Island and Its People*, 3:15.
664. "Staten Island Independent. She Has Golden Prospects and Prefers Not to Take Chances," *New York Herald*, March 17, 1889.

665. Ibid.
666. "Will Canada Join the Union? She May Some Day, Erastus Wiman Tells the Senate Committee, but Prefers Commercial Union First," *New York Herald*, December 31, 1889.
667. "Staten Island Independent."
668. Ibid.
669. Ibid.
670. "Mayor Gleason's Bailiwick. Long Island City's Chief Magistrate in Favor of Annexation—Others Opposed," *New York Herald*, March 17, 1889.
671. "Westchester's Opposition. Her Leading Citizens Strongly Object to the Proposed Annexation," *New York Herald*, March 17, 1889.
672. "Various Views from Brooklyn. Mr. Stranahan Favors Annexation—Other Citizens Oppose It," *New York Herald*, March 17, 1889.
673. "Greater New-York Debated. Mr. Crosby's Bill Ordered to Third Reading in the Assembly," *New York Tribune*, April 5, 1889.
674. Hammack, *Power and Society*, 194.
675. Kaplan, "Andrew H. Green," 38.
676. Burrows and Wallace, *Gotham*, 1,228.
677. Kaplan, "Andrew H. Green," 38.
678. Hammack, *Power and Society*, 195.
679. Ibid.
680. "The Legislative Caldron. Latest Aspects of the Inside Situation at Albany," *New York Herald*, February 16, 1885.
681. "Albany Gossip. Governor Hill's Fruitless Listening—General Carr—The Lobbyists," *New York Tribune*, May 12, 1885.
682. Hammack, *Power and Society*, 195.
683. Ibid.
684. "To Be or Not Be One Municipality. How the State Senators Stand on the Great Annexation Question," *New York Herald*, October 4, 1890.
685. Chapter 311, *Laws of the State of New York, Passed at the One Hundred and Thirteenth Session of the Legislature, Begun January Sixth, 1890, and Ended May Ninth, 1890, in the City of Albany* (Albany, NY: Banks & Brothers, Publishers, 1890), 597–98.
686. "Annexation Commission Confirmed. Mr. Jacobs Tries Obstruction—The Harvey Claim Bill Beaten," *New York Tribune*, May 10, 1890.
687. "Behold New York the Greater! Glimpses at the Metropolis of the World as It Will Look in 1950," *New York Herald*, May 18, 1890.
688. Morris, *Morris's Memorial History of Staten Island*, 2:489.
689. Hammack, *Power and Society*, 196.

690. "Mr. Green Defeated. Failure of His Consolidation Resolutions," *New York Tribune*, March 28, 1891.
691. Kaplan, "Andrew H. Green," 38.
692. Ibid., 39.
693. "For a 'Greater New York.' The Municipal Consolidation Inquiry Commission Meet and Have Some Plain Talk," *New York Herald*, June 2, 1892.
694. "Up Looms Greater New York. Brooklyn Citizens Insist Upon a Popular Vote Upon Consolidation," *New York Herald*, October 7, 1892.
695. "Brooklyn's Alternative. E.C. Grave's Argument for Consolidation. What Erastus Wiman and Orlando B. Potter Say," *New York Tribune*, April 3, 1891.
696. Leng and Davis, *Staten Island and Its People*, 2:558.
697. "For a Greater New-York. The Consolidation Commission Draws Up a Bill," *New York Tribune*, December 13, 1893.
698. "Greater New-York. A Bill Authorizing a Charter Sent to Albany. The Municipal Consolidation Commission Listens to Advice—Mr. Curtis's Doubts," *New York Tribune*, April 7, 1891.
699. Kaplan, "Andrew H. Green," 39.
700. Ibid.
701. Burrows and Wallace, *Gotham*, 1,228.
702. Hammack, *Power and Society*, 198.
703. Graves, *Greater New York*, 5.
704. George J. Greenfield, "Greater New York. How Consolidation Would Decrease Our Taxes," *Staten Island Independent*, November 2, 1894.
705. Ibid.
706. Burrows and Wallace, *Gotham*, 1,230–31.
707. Untitled editorial, *Richmond County Advance*, February 24, 1894.
708. Burrows and Wallace, *Gotham*, 1,231.
709. *Report and Proceedings of the Senate Committee Appointed to Investigate the Police Department of the City of New York*, vol. 1 (Albany, NJ: James B. Lyon, State Printer, 1895). Nearly every one of the dozens of witness throughout the report described these incidents in explicit detail.
710. "Money Paid to Captains. So the Witnesses Testify," *New York Tribune*, June 5, 1894.
711. "Telling What They Paid," *New York Tribune*, June 5, 1894.
712. "The Lexow Committee's Discoveries," *New York Tribune*, June 5, 1894.
713. "Vote Consolidation Down This Year!," *Brooklyn Daily Eagle*, November 2, 1894.

714. "A Ring to Be Smashed. Work that Should Be Done on Staten Island To-Day," *New York Tribune*, November 6, 1894.

715. Untitled editorial, *Richmond County Advance*, February 24, 1894.

716. Graves, *Greater New York*, 15.

717. Shaw, quoted in Burrows and Wallace, *Gotham*, 1,230.

718. "The Real Machine Ticket," *Staten Island Independent*, November 2, 1894.

719. "For Political Redemption. Richmond County's Opportunity Will Come To-Morrow," *New York Tribune*, November 5, 1894.

720. George J. Greenfield, "To the People of Richmond County," *Staten Island Independent*, October 27, 1894.

721. "Richmond Leads," *Staten Island Independent*, November 13, 1894.

722. Leng and Davis, *Staten Island and Its People*, 1:331, 5:144.

723. Charles L. Benedict, *Appt. v. United States*, 176 U.S. 357 (1900).

724. Leng and Davis, *Staten Island and Its People*, 1:331, 3:206.

725. Zeta Psi Fraternity, "Satterlee, Livingston," *Zeta Psi Fraternity of North America. Founded June 1 Anno Domini 1847. Semicentennial Biographical Catalogue with Data to December 31 1899* (New York: Published for the Fraternity, 1900), 295.

726. Leng and Davis, *Staten Island and Its People*, 1:331, 4:418.

727. Tysen, *Happenings Before and After*, 14.

728. Kaplan, "Andrew H. Green," 39.

729. Foord, *Life and Public Services of Andrew Haswell Green*, 191.

730. "The People Do Rule. Total Vote of the Towns on All Candidates and Measures," *Staten Island Independent*, November 9, 1894.

731. "Staten Island Free. Nicholas Muller's Notorious Ring Broken. The Honest People of Richmond County Rise," *New York Tribune*, November 7, 1894.

732. "People Do Rule."

733. Kaplan, "Andrew H. Green," 39.

734. Hammack, *Power and Society*, 214.

735. "Progress and Fall of Platt, Easy Boss," *New York Times*, March 3, 1910.

736. Burrows and Wallace, *Gotham*, 1,233–34.

737. "Will Oust Muller. New Police Bill Introduced in the Assembly," *Staten Island Independent*, January 22, 1895.

738. "Citizen Candidate for Supervisor, Town of Northfield, Edward P. Doyle," advertisement, *Staten Island Independent*, February 8, 1895.

739. "New Board of Supervisors," *Staten Island Independent*, February 15, 1895.

740. Ibid.

741. "New Brighton Emancipated," *Staten Island Independent*, July 12, 1895.

742. "Supervisor Doyle," *Staten Island Independent*, July 12, 1895.

743. Editorial, *Richmond County Advance*, March 28, 1896.

744. Burrows and Wallace, *Gotham*, 1,233–34.

745. Leng and Davis, *Staten Island and Its People*, 1:331.

746. "All Sorts," *Staten Island Independent*, February 8, 1895.

747. Leng and Davis, *Staten Island and Its People*, 1:331; Hammack, *Power and Society*, 225.

748. Gerald Kurland, *Seth Low: The Reformer in an Urban and Industrial Age* (New York: Twayne Publishers Inc., 1971), 78–79.

749. Hammack, *Power and Society*, 225–26.

750. Morris, *Morris's Memorial History of Staten Island*, 2:491.

751. Hammack, *Power and Society*, 226.

752. James. W. Pryor, "The Greater New York Charter: The Formation of the Charter," *The Annals of the American Academy of Political and Social Science* 10 (July 1897): 20–32, 32.

753. Ibid.

754. Mike Wallace, *Greater Gotham: A History of New York City from 1898 to 1919* (New York: Oxford University Press, 2017), 55–56.

755. Ibid.

756. "The Tammany Convention," *New York Tribune*, October 1, 1897.

757. Ibid.

758. "Nominations in Richmond," *New York Tribune*, October 8, 1897.

759. "Mr. Croker and Mr. Bryan Interesting Situation Reported in the Democratic Club," *New York Tribune*, January 5, 1898.

760. "The Democratic Convention Called to Meet on Thursday, September 30," *New York Tribune*, September 4, 1897.

761. "Now for the Supervisors," *Staten Island Independent*, November 13, 1894.

762. "Erastus Wiman on Prosperity. A Discussion on the Average Condition of Workingmen to Be Held," *New York Tribune*, September 11, 1897.

763. "Staten Island Happenings," *New York Tribune*, October 16, 1897.

764. "The Local Candidates. Men to Be Voted for in the New City. A Complete List," *New York Tribune*, November 1, 1897.

765. Ibid.

766. "Up-State Opinion," *New York Tribune*, September 7, 1897.

767. Wallace, *Greater Gotham*, 56.

768. "Mr. Quigg Reiterates. No Indorsement [*sic*] of Low by the Republicans," *New York Tribune*, September 7, 1897.
769. Ibid.
770. "Woodruff Favors Union. He Thinks Tracy Win in a Four-Cornered Contest," *New York Tribune*, October 4, 1897.
771. "The Tammany Ticket. Exceptionally Weak," *New York Tribune*, October 4, 1897.
772. "Letters to the Editor: The Plain Duty of Republicans," *New York Tribune*, October 14, 1897.
773. "Gen. Tracy in Brooklyn. His Hearers Cheer Low," *New York Tribune*, October 12, 1897.
774. "Republicans for Low. Magnificent Mass Meeting. Demonstrations for the Citizens Candidate in Carnegie Hall," *New York Tribune*, October 22, 1897.
775. "Course of the Betting. Two to One on Low Against Tracy—A Bet of $1,200," *New York Tribune*, October 27, 1897.
776. Wallace, *Greater Gotham*, 56.
777. "The Machines in Accord. Every Effort Will Be Made to Defeat Low," *The Tribune*, October 27, 1897.
778. "Partners," *New York Tribune*, October 23, 1897.
779. "The Local Candidates. Men to Be Voted for in the New City. A Complete List," *New York Tribune*, November 1, 1897.
780. "Gen. Tracy Formally Named. He Accepts, but Will Not Stand in the Way of Anti-Tammany," *New York Tribune*, September 29, 1897.
781. "To Usurp All Power. The Machine's Scheme for Abolishing the County Committees. Republican Politicians Awaking," *New York Tribune*, October 2, 1897.
782. "Mr. Low on Staten Island Addressing Audiences at Stapleton and Prohibition Park. A Hearty Welcome," *New York Tribune*, October 29, 1897.
783. "Prohibition Park Was Rooted in Temperance," *Staten Island Advance*, October 24, 2010.
784. "Mr. Low on Staten Island."
785. Ibid.
786. Ibid.
787. Ibid.
788. "Democratic City, Borough, and County Tickets Are Elected," *New York Times*, November 3, 1897.
789. "Tammany Sweeps the City, Robert A. Van Wyck Chosen First Mayor of the Greater New York," *New York Tribune*, November 3, 1897.

790. "The Triumph of the Tiger," *New York Tribune*, November 3, 1897.
791. "Tammany Sweeps the City."
792. "Democrats Take All," *New York Times*, November 4, 1897.
793. "Filling Up the Offices. The Patronage Mill Still Grinding Out Appointments for Tammany Men," *New York Times*, January 5, 1898.
794. "Political Drift. Cromwell President of Richmond. The Board of Canvassers to Give Him the Certificate," *New York Tribune*, November 19, 1897.
795. "Dr. Feeny Gets the Office. The Richmond Canvassers Declare Him Elected President of the Borough—Mr. Cromwell to Fight," *New York Times*, December 17, 1897; "Dr. Feeny Declared Elected. Justice Dykman Decides Contest in Favor of the Democratic Candidate," *New York Tribune*, December 17, 1897.
796. "Dr. Feeny Declared Elected."
797. "Gains for Cromwell. The Appellate Division Admits Votes for Him that Were Declared Void by Justice Dykman," *New York Tribune*, December 28, 1897.
798. "D.B. Hill and Chief Judge Parker," *New York Tribune*, February 8, 1898.
799. "Cromwell Declared Elected. The Appellate Division Decides the Contested Election in Richmond Borough in Favor of the Republican Candidate," *New York Tribune*, December 30, 1897.
800. Ibid.
801. "No President of Richmond. Justice Van Wyck Does Not Interfere in the Legal Proceedings," *New York Tribune*, January 1, 1898.
802. "Farewell to City, Hail to Borough," *Brooklyn Daily Eagle*, January 2, 1898.
803. "Ceremonies in Brooklyn. Union Quietly Observed by a Reception in City Hall by the Mayor and Ex-Mayors. Orators Praise the Old City," *New York Times*, January 1, 1898.
804. "Van Wyck at the Helm. He Takes Charge of the New City's Government with Practically No Ceremony," *New York Times*, January 2, 1898.
805. Plunkitt, as quoted in Wallace, *Greater Gotham*, 60.
806. William Safire, "honest graft," in *Safire's Political Dictionary* (New York: Oxford University Press, 2008), 322.
807. "Van Wyck at the Helm."
808. Tysen, *Happenings Before and After*, 9; "Staten Island Happenings," *New York Tribune*, January 1, 1898.

809. "Staten Island Happenings," *New York Tribune*, January 1, 1898.
810. Ibid.
811. "No President of Richmond."
812. "Cromwell Declared Elected."
813. "President Cromwell Barred. The Board of Public Improvements Declines to Honor His Credentials," *New York Tribune*, June 2, 1898.
814. "Cromwell's Name Not Yet on the Roll. The Board of Public Improvement Decides to Wait," *New York Tribune*, June 23, 1898.
815. "President Cromwell Seated. Takes His Place with the Board of Public Improvements—No Penalties for Contractors," *New York Tribune*, June 30, 1898.
816. "To Certify Cromwell's Election," *New York Tribune*, July 1, 1898.
817. "Richmond Borough Happenings," *New York Tribune*, August 29, 1898.

Epilogue

818. "Robert A. Van Wyck Dies in Paris Home," *New York Times*, November 16, 1918.
819. Bird S. Coler, "The Government of Greater New York," *North American Review* 169, no. 512 (July 1899): 90–100, 91.
820. Tysen, *Happenings Before and After*, 16–17.
821. Ibid., 27–28.
822. Ibid., 35.
823. Amisha Padnani, "A Subway to Staten Island? How a Transit Dream Died," *New York Times*, January 18, 2019.
824. *Mayor Hylan Breaking Ground for Richmond—Brooklyn Tunnel*, July 1923, Staten Island Geographic Collection, Staten Island Historical Society, Staten Island, New York.
825. Padnani, "Subway to Staten Island?"
826. "Proposal to Secede from the City Assailed," *New York Times*, January 12, 1947.
827. Craig Schneider and Carl Campanile, "65% Say YES to Independence," *Staten Island Advance*, November 3, 1993.
828. Jeffrey Kroessler, "The Limits of Liberal Planning: The Lindsay Administration's Failed Plan to Control Development on Staten Island," *Journal of Planning History* 16, no. 4 (November 2017): 263–84, 265–78.
829. Kramer and Flanagan, *Staten Island*, 99.

About the Author

Joseph Borelli is a member and minority leader of the New York City Council, representing the south shore of Staten Island since 2015. He also served as the chairman of the council's committee on fire and emergency management, which has oversight over the FDNY and the office of Emergency Management. Prior to this, he was a member of the New York State Assembly, representing the Sixty-Second District of Staten Island between 2013 and 2015. Joe is also an adjunct professor of political science at the College of Staten Island and was a Lindsay Fellow at the CUNY Institute of State and Local Governance. He is a contributor to *The Hill* and regularly appears as a commentator on Fox News, Fox Business, CNN, CNNI, HLN, BBC, OAN, AM970 and WABC. He has also been published in the *New York Daily News*, *New York Post*, *Washington Times*, *Washington Examiner*, *Staten Island Advance*, *Gotham Gazette* and *City and State NY*. He serves as a spokesman for the New York State Republican Party. Joe received a BA in history from Marist College and an MA in history from the College of Staten Island at the City University of New York. He lives in Annadale with his wife, Rachel; two sons, Joseph Jr. and John; and an overweight English bulldog named Luna.

Visit us at
www.historypress.com